PRAISE FOR *BEING BREAD*

Stephen Muse's finely written book is full of profound insights, eyebrow-raising surprises and unforgettable stories. He adds new depths to a sentence most of us pray at least once daily, "Give us this day our daily bread."

> **Jim Forest**
> author of *St. George and the Dragon*; *All Is Grace*; *For the Peace From Above*

Stephen's musings reveal in the sweetness of his story-telling a vivid aliveness to the Spirit's presence and action in a receptive heart. He shares with deep vulnerability his inner dialogues between ego and Spirit, and his moments of wonder at exploring "how far will I go to meet others and myself in God?" With delight and laughter, tenderness and gratitude, Stephen offers us a multicultural stew of "glimmerings of Divine gifts," served as a relish to the main course of "being Bread." Rarely is the depth of God's love of the cosmos and of each of us tasted so enjoyably.

> **Dr. Demetra Velisarios Jaquet, D.Min.**
> Clinical Director,
> Rocky Mountain Center for Spiritual Caregivers

How can we become again like little children - with open hearts free of the numbness and guile that so infects us as adults - to become aware of God's continuing presence, filling our lives with beauty and meaning? This book points the way and shows us the path we must follow. The reader will soon discover that Christ is there at the beginning of our journey, accompanies us along the way — and is indeed the path itself — and waits for us with open arms at the end of our journey. Here is a book rich with insight into being able to see the extraordinary in the ordinary, the sacramental and therefore relational nature of everyone and everything — and the consequences of this vision for how we ought to live as believers.

Fr. Steven Tsichlis
St. Paul's Greek Orthodox Church, Irvine, CA

This inspiring book will help many people break out of their customary way of viewing life. The questions at the end of each chapter do not let the reader be merely content with enjoying the insightful ideas, but they gently invite a deeper look within. It would be a good thing for people to read before going to confession!

Hieromonk Ephraim

Pouring over these sustaining narratives, these portions of bread for the journey — τὸν ἄρτον ἡμῶν τὸν ἐπιούσιον — I startled to joyful recognition at having come upon another brother along the way, one who is being drawn along the journey of prayer, which is also the journey to prayer, which is abundant life in Christ. Δόξα τῷ Θεῷ!!"

Scott Cairns
author of *Slow Pilgrim* (originally *Short Trip to the Edge*)

Being Bread

Other books by this author:

Beside Still Waters: Resources for Shepherds in the Market Place, Macon, GA: Smyth & Helwys (2000).

Raising Lazarus: Integral Healing in Orthodox Christianity, Brookline, MA: Holy Cross Orthodox Press (2004).

When Hearts Become Flame: An Eastern Orthodox Approach to the διά-Λογος of Pastoral Counseling, Rollinsford, NH: Orthodox Research Institute (2011).

Other books published by the Orthodox Research Institute include:

Fr. David G. Bissias. *The Mystery of Healing: Oil, Anointing, and the Unity of the Local Church*

Byron J. Gaist, Ph.D. *Creative Suffering and the Wounded Healer: Analytical Psychology and Orthodox Christian Theology*

Alphonse and Rachel Goettmann. *The Spiritual Wisdom and Practices of Early Christianity*

Archimandrite Kyprian Kern. *Orthodox Pastoral Service.* Edited by Fr. William C. Mills

Jean-Claude Larchet. *Life after Death according to the Orthodox Church*

Fr. William C. Mills (ed.). *Called to Serve: Readings on Ministry from the Orthodox Church*

Vladimir Moss. *The Theology of Eros*

Rt. Rev. Dr. Archimandrite Andrew (Vujisić). *Orthodox Interventions: Orthodox Neptic Psychotherapy in Response to Existential and Transpersonal Psychology*

Being Bread

Stephen Muse, Ph.D.

ORTHODOX
RESEARCH
INSTITUTE
Rollinsford, New Hampshire

Published by Orthodox Research Institute
20 Silver Lane
Rollinsford, NH 03869
www.orthodoxresearchinstitute.org

ISBN 978-1-933275-65-9

A person is always a gift from someone.
Metropolitan John Zizioulas

Our birth and then our development on earth is nothing other than a creative process during the course of which we acquire being to the degree available to us in the hope that knowledge only half gained here will be completed beyond the boundaries of this form of our existence.
Archimandrite Sophrony

*The **true bread** is that which nourishes the true humanity, the person created after the image of God.*
Origen

Jesus said, "I am the living bread that came down from heaven; if anyone eats of this bread, he will live forever; and the bread that I shall give is my flesh for the life of the world."
John 6:51

Table of Contents

Acknowledgments

A BOOK COMES INTO BEING WITH ENCOUR-
agement and perspectives from many voices. I want to
express my gratefulness to Fr. Vasileios Thermos and Lea
Povozhaev for their encouragement and Natasha Kes-
meti and Matushka Deborah Belonick for their helpful
editorial suggestions on how to improve the writing as
well as the organization of the book. A special thank you
to Hieromonk Ephraim for his attention to numerous
details in the manuscript. Finally, to my wife Claudia,
whose sacrifices of labor allow me the time to write and
whose love has given me reason to want to. I thank you.

454 South Lorraine Blvd.
Los Angeles, CA 90020
www.antiochianladiocese.org

Office: 323 934-3131
Fax: 323 934-1389
bishopjoseph@antiochianladiocese.org

Antiochian Orthodox Christian Archdiocese of North America
The Diocese of Los Angeles and the West

His Eminence, Archbishop JOSEPH

November 14, 2012

Beloved in Christ:

Ancient spiritual wisdom can be stated: Know thyself. One condition afflicting modern man in his high-tech, industrial and urban world is spiritual schizophrenia: the heart and head are divided from each other. A serious spiritual disorder! Here is a welcome and profitable contribution to Orthodox Christian devotional literature, a primer toward self-knowledge.

When one thinks of theology or spiritual literature, the idea of a dense, hard-to-understand, and compact prose comes to mind. We need reminders that good theology is expressed in experiences of divine Grace, and that these experiences are conveyed through stories and dialogues, especially through personal encounters with others. This is why the lives the saints serve us so well; we are in contact with the life-experience of the saint.

Dr. Muse's book gives us experiential, every day encounters, happenings, thoughts, and dialogues to reflect on for our profit. He organizes his book into 25 short vignettes, each consisting of a few pages easily read in one sitting. At the end of each vignette a few questions serve to provoke the reader's own personal questions, especially in provocative ways leading to deeper self-knowledge, and above all, to the kind of knowledge most helpful for achieving soul-saving repentance!

Frequently, we encourage penitents to use questions for training in self-examination, something easily found in pocket prayerbooks and the like. But, something more probing is frequently needed, and Muse's offering of love serves well in this regard. For example, in "Pascha in July," when we encounter St. Basil's word, "The bread you do not use is the bread of the hungry. The garment hanging in your wardrobe is the garment of the person who is naked ...," it would be easy to say, "amen!" and head off into our day not further affected. But Dr. Muse presents us with the question, "How many pairs of shoes are in my closet? ... Do I become less greedy the more I have?" Faithful Christians will find great personal profit through these engrossing contemporary stories combined with the Christian actions they stimulate.

Yours in Christ,

[signature]

+ ARCHBISHOP JOSEPH
Diocese of Los Angeles and the West
Antiochian Orthodox Christian Archdiocese of North America

Introduction

STUDENTS IN THE SERVANT LEADERSHIP masters program of Columbus State University invited some community leaders to a conversation on the theme "Embracing the Beauty around Us." During lunch, we gathered in one of the studios on the riverfront campus where we were shown a film taken from cameras installed in the Washington DC Metro at a time when celebrated concert violinist, Joshua Bell, agreed to play several haunting and incredibly difficult pieces of music.[1] Dressed incognito in a baseball cap with an open violin case beside him, standing off to the side against a wall, he played his 300-year-old Stradivarius violin for nearly 40 minutes, collecting thirty dollars in donations in the process. Predictions had been that hundreds of people would stop to listen to the virtuoso, but the cameras recorded the sobering

[1] Readers can find a fuller account in *The Washington Post* article by Gene Wiengarten, Sunday April 8, 2007, W 10.

truth that of some 1,100 people passing by that morning, only seven stopped to listen.

Most of those who did stop, or tried to, were children who were captivated simply by the music itself.[2] They were most vulnerable to the actual *presence* of beauty for its own sake, when not framed by the obvious attire of the maestro in Alpert Hall with all the trappings of an 'evening sold out' at $150 a ticket, which appeals to the cultured, worldly, social ego. These children had no interest in all that. They were without guile. Noticing the incongruity of this joyful music hidden quietly and unobtrusively in a corner of the Washington metro on an ordinary everyday run-of-the-mill workaday morning, the children actively struggled with their hypnotized parents. They tried to turn them aside like Moses, to respond to the hidden fire that was setting their hearts aflame without burning them.

Unresponsive, their parents would not permit them to take off their shoes on this profane ground. They were not allowed, even for a few seconds, just to be still and listen. Held captive to the inertia of another morning ritual en route to meeting the various obligations of a day which did not include the freedom to notice and attend to "a new thing," these parents were not vulnerable to being awak- .

---

[2] Seven year old Edward Yudenich conducts the student orchestra of the State Conservatoire of Uzbekistan. This is pure joy to watch — a testimony to the child's potential to recognize and respond to beauty. http://www.youtube.com/watch_popup?v=BNNFtlF9CDE.

ened to beauty by their children's as yet unsullied capacity to be touched by it. Not only did they miss being refreshed by this gratuitous blessing, they forfeited the gift of seeing their children's pure attention and guileless hearts, calling them in a different direction, if only for a moment, where they might have received an unexpected nourishment capable of transforming their whole day.

Like Balaam,[3] they did not notice the angel in front of them. Why could they not discern the difference between their children's disobedient tug and the miracle of their response to an angelic summons, stopping them in their tracks, dissolving the hypnotic monotony of the familiar morning ritual? The parents did not hear the music, or if they did, they did not *value* it. What had happened to their hearts? They could not see through their children's eyes or hear through their children's ears. They were not *present*. And they were teaching their children to become like them, deaf, dumb, and blind to spontaneous personal encounter. Gratefulness for the pristine newness of every moment is given to us like *manna*[4] wherever there is *presence* to receive it. Vulnerability to the felt awareness

---

[3] Cf. Num. 22:21–38. A prophet, Balaam, is unable to see the angel blocking the road in front him, but his donkey sees it and tries to go around. Balaam tugs against him and strikes him and cries out that he wishes that he had a sword to strike the donkey for being disobedient! At that moment, God makes the donkey speak and he reveals that an angel is blocking the path in front of them. Then Balaam also sees the angel standing with a fiery sword and he repents.

[4] Literally, in Hebrew, "What is it?"

of one's own *being in relationship* is an essential ingredient. Standing before the great I AM, the Giver of life, all life becomes Eucharist[5] that transforms the quality of our impressions. What we receive in this way is raised to another level, just as bread and wine become the Body and Blood of Christ, though remaining bread and wine. When we receive these elements with discernment of the relationship that unites heaven and earth, they become nourishment for our *being*. "Give us today our daily *being* bread"[6] is a prayer to God that we may receive all the

---

[5] The Greek work *Eucharist* means thanksgiving as well as refers to the Body of Christ who unites heaven and earth.

[6] The Greek word in the Lord's Prayer usually translated into English as "daily" is ἐπιούσιον. According to Origen, St. Gregory Nyssa, and others, this word is something of a neologism, a combination of επί, meaning 'beyond' or 'above', and οὐσία, the word for essence or 'being'. In other words, it serves as a modifier for the word bread (ἄρτον). In this sense, the phrase "our daily bread" should be rendered to convey a meaning that includes being nourished "beyond our physical being" by God. It takes on Eucharistic overtones referring to the bread of heaven which is Christ. In Latin, it was translated as "super-substantial" bread. I am choosing the word *being* to emphasize this Eucharistic relationship that is essential nourishment for humanity who in fact cannot live by bread alone. Our most important nourishment is the living person of God. While this refers to the mystery of the transformation of the coinherence of bread and wine and the Body and Blood of Christ through the power of the Holy Spirit, it goes beyond this to include the mystery of how created human beings are transformed into vessels of the Holy Spirit, bearers of the Uncreated Light, on a daily basis. The encounter between God and humanity is reciprocal and personal: God becomes human and humans are infused with the Divine life wherever we are truly *present* to the *other*.

world and one another as Eucharist, on a daily basis and become *Eucharist* ourselves for others.

The prologue of the Gospel according to St. John[7] declares that God the *Logos,* whose life is the light that enlightens humankind, became flesh and dwelled among us. Strangely, He came to His own in human form and His own did not receive Him. But those who did, received nourishment for their *being* that was not born of this earth or of flesh and blood or of emotional desire and human will. The strange paradox of this opportunity for διά-Λογος[8] continues in our lives every day in the midst of ordinary events. How do we cultivate within us a capacity for vulnerability to have ears to hear and eyes to see Him who is hidden in the midst of us in and through the people, places and events we encounter every day?

The students posed three questions to the group of invitees: "Where do we find beauty and meaning in our lives? What beauty is going unnoticed or being ignored and why? How can we be more like the children in the video and recognize and appreciate beauty more read-

---

[7] Jn. 1:1–14.

[8] διά-Λογος from the Greek "dia," meaning "through," and the Greek word "Logos," which is used for God the Son by the Apostle John in the opening lines of the Gospel, refers to the mysterious intersection between the created world and the uncreated through Christ who is the ground for the possibility of every transformative personal encounter of this kind. Cf. S. Muse. *When Hearts Become Flame: An Eastern Orthodox Approach to the διά-Λογος of Pastoral Counseling* (Rollinsford, NH: Orthodox Research Institute, 2011).

ily?" They were not thinking Eucharist. As is often the case, beauty itself seemed enough to hope for. But if, indeed, as Dostoevsky says, "Beauty will save the world," it is because beauty arises only in the *presence* of love. Without love there is nothing beautiful. There is nothing valuable. There is nothing meaningful. God is revealed to us as love between the call and response of personal encounter. Yet, the monologue of egoism, like a certain creature "more subtle than all the rest,"[9] is always inviting us to prefer the gifts over the Giver, to seek to own or merely to name and know about the world, rather than to be vulnerable to God and each other through relationship with it.

I *am* only because *Thou* art. To be an "I" without personal relationship with a "Thou" is merely to exist, to be a thing, refusing to partake of the bread of heaven which alone renders us human. It is to have a heart of stone, instead of a heart of flesh. Such egocentricity is the worst imaginable hell. We mark the passing of our lives along the dusty road of linear time, which is *chronos*, all the while longing to eat from the tree of eternal life that originates from outside time and beyond the created order. This is *kairos*, where meaning arises and transformation occurs. The created and uncreated worlds cross along the path of personal encounter where we discover a third presence Who awakens us from the determinism and inertia of biological life. Lifting every moment up to

---

[9] Gen. 3:1.

be blessed and offered back as gift, we discover that the smallest crumb has potential to nourish in such a way that "all are satisfied,"[10] and still there is abundance remaining.

We eat our daily bread to sustain biological life, but it is the uncreated encounters of faith in love coming through the call and response of our life together in Christ that nourish our being unto eternal life. The personal encounters and theological reflections in this volume, along with the study questions that follow each section, are offered in celebration of Him who, in surprising ways and unexpected circumstances, becomes the precious and pure gift of our daily *being* bread so that we may learn together the mystery of becoming bread for others in return. I wish this for all who read this book.

> Sunday of the Holy Myrrh Bearers and
> St. John the Evangelist
> May 8, 2011
> Columbus, Georgia

---

[10] Mk. 6:42.

Harumbai!

Those of us who wish to gain understanding must never stop examining ourselves, and if, in the perception of your soul, you realize that your neighbor is superior to you in all respects, then the mercy of God is surely near at hand.
St. John Climacus

MY COLLEAGUE JOHN INVITED ME TO ATTEND a Lenten luncheon at one of the downtown churches. Unbeknownst to me, they were doing a four part series on the Lord's Prayer, and this session was to be on "Give us this day our daily bread."

I agreed to go with him, although in my mind I imagined it as a public grip and grin event that is something I generally like to avoid. I would rather take my lunch quietly in a corner somewhere nibbling on a few pages of St. Maximos the Confessor, a poem or two of Rumi or with a friend who can be still and have a conversation of depth that is without compulsion, open the shared mystery between us.

We paid our five dollars and got in the food line. I skipped the meat portion, aware of the Lenten fast, and looked out over the sea of tables of well-dressed and comfortable upper class men and women. Many of the movers and shakers of the community were present. Over in a corner, sat a disheveled obese woman in a wheelchair with plastic tubes under her nose from an oxygen tank. There was only one other person at her table. I sat down beside her.

She was deeply immersed in her lunch, relishing the chicken soup I had refused. "You gotta try this soup!" she says in her husky, grainy voice, as soon as I sit down. "This is the best soup I've had in a long time. You gotta try this soup. It's greeaatt!"

I thank her, and before I have even finished declining her invitation, she repeats it again, not to persuade me, but more as a declaration of joy and guileless exuberance. I learn later she does not have money to buy food, so she comes to the church often to eat. She lives by herself in the city in an apartment for people with little or no income. "This soup is greeaat!" she says again." I smile and nod, without a clue at that point what it might mean to her. Then she says it again as if I did not hear her the first two times.

Her gleeful insistence on the soup's *greaaatness* conjures up the old animated cartoon character Tony the Tiger from my childhood cereal commercials. I imagine his booming voice joining the chorus. Then my attention was caught by the salad which was quite good, with small fruits and glazed nuts scattered in it and an especially tasty herbal dressing. The flavors are definitely much better quality than the usual church soup kitchen fare. Subtle unique combinations evidence how someone has taken special care to prepare it.

Engrossed in my own eating now and thoughts about what is going on around the room, I did not notice this large woman beside me had slipped away from the table in her wheelchair. As she wheeled herself back, I discovered that she had been on an errand of mercy to bring me a bowl of that soup! Not to be deterred, this time I touch her lightly on the arm in an intentionally friendly way and tell her "I'm not eating soup, I'm a vegetarian." I am feeling inwardly uncomfortable as I say these words which are a deliberate lie, refusing this soul's gift obtained at her initiative and sacrifice in order to care for the strange man beside her who has clearly not got his eyes, nose and heart on what is important. Only those who have been hungry and who do not enjoy the privilege of never having to wonder if they will be able to get food know its real value. These are also the ones who have learned the necessity of sharing what makes for life with others whose life may also depend on another's generosity.

"I am too!" she says, "But this soup is greeaat! You'll love it!" I take the soup, though I still have not decided to eat it. The awareness of the reversal that has just taken place is still dawning in my mind, its significance gnawing away at a deeper resistance in me. It is a resistance to Grace born of a place in the heart that has not yet learned to share, but only to willfully approximate love. Eventually, the foundations of my high and mightiness crumble, and I eat the soup feeling I need to explain to my inner vainglorious, self-justifying press secretary posing as god, that because it is a gift from her it would be a greater wrong to reject it. Straining at gnats ...

By this time, I have already eaten one piece of apple sauce cake from the desert plate that was so delicious I could easily have morphed into Tony the Tiger about *it*! I wanted another piece, but inwardly listened to the commentary in my head saying, "You don't have to be a glutton. You have already eaten the soup with chicken in it. If you truly want to be obedient and honor the fast, don't eat a second piece of that cake." So I agree. Regretfully. I sip on sweet tea and congratulate myself for having made a good choice. It is a kind of consolation and that in itself reveals that I do not so much take joy in obeying the Lord, as I relish the reward of compulsive obedience for the sake of being congratulated by the audience of one in myself as *special* for having done so.

Still in touch with greediness taking hold in me, it does not escape my attention a few minutes later when the plate of apple sauce cake is being passed around the table. I expect all the pieces to be taken and entertain the thought that this will prove that if I had eaten a second piece, there would not have been enough for everyone.

When the plate gets to the obese woman beside me with the strong repugnant body odor I have now begun to notice, she holds it out to me with one dimpled arm. I demure. She is not one to take no for an answer and barks in that curiously atonal, yet somehow dispassionate insistently husky voice, "My arm's gett'n tired!" So I take the cake, a little sunrise of anticipation rising within my palate.

The second piece is probably as good as the first, but for some reason I eat it faster this time, hardly noticing the taste. My soul lacks the presence necessary truly to savor and appreciate the experience of eating the cake, dominated more by hunger for pleasure and because my attention is now diverted to pondering the choices I am making and what is happening around me.

Oddly enough, I had prayed earlier this morning that I really wanted to be attentive today and to have an encounter with God. It was a sincere prayer born of the hope from the previous evening's prayer in which I had felt silence deepen on its own and fill with the mystery of the world as *gift*. I wanted to return to this today in some way, so I specifically asked God for help, with hope in the guilelessness of the request. But now, wrapped in the drama of the unfolding events, I had forgotten all about that earlier prayer. Wrapped up and distracted by a thousand little strands of passionate thoughts, like Gulliver surrounded by the Lilliputians, I was more immobilized than I realized.

It was now time for the speaker. An older red-faced southern clergyman is introduced to us by the polished young rector of the local parish. I think to myself that he has probably drunk too much sherry in his day, schmoozing and coddling the well-to-do for so long that he is not going to do anything with this crowd but give them a few laughs and present the Gospel in a way that further affirms their social standing and privilege.

Sure enough, he starts off with a story about Harlan Sanders and how he burned down three of his stores and got the insurance to build new ones and then after he began to make some money he got an audience with the Pope and said, "Your Holiness, I'll give you 10 million dollars if you'll change the words to the Lord's Prayer from 'Give us our daily bread' to 'Give us our daily chicken!'"

The Pope politely declined, like me and the apple sauce cake. So Harlan went back home and made a ton more money. One day he got another audience with the Pope and said, "Your Holiness, I'll give you 500 million dollars if you'll change the line in the Lord's Prayer from 'Give us our daily bread,' to 'Give us our daily chicken.'" This time the Pope was less thoughtful and said, "Why thank you. Harlan, I mean Colonel. I think we can do that."

So he calls a conclave and tells his cardinals, "I've got some good news and some bad news. The good news is that Harlan Sanders is going to give the Church a half billion dollars." That was a lot back in those days! The cardinals all nod their heads approvingly. "Now for the bad news," the Pope continues, "We lost the Wonder Bread account."

Everybody in the room titters and roars with appreciative laughter, and my suspicions are quietly confirmed that this old fellow knows exactly how to tend these pedigreed sheep and not get thrown out on his ear. He goes on in a casual and cultured southern story teller's cultivated spontaneity, born of many such talks, and regales the group with humor and casual repartee, interacting with one or two in order to emphasize the point with engaging gestures that "You can't 'give' something unless it's yours to give."

Slowly he is making the case that "our daily bread" is not ours, but God's and that is why we have to *ask* for it. I am wondering how this will go down with the corporate folks at the top of the food chain earning disproportionately large amounts off the backs of the poorest 70% of the people. The top one percent of the population's income has tripled over the past 30 years, while the rest has been flat. Those on minimum wage have lost about 60% through inflation.

I am only mildly paying attention as I reflect on these inequities when all of a sudden he does a U turn. "I learned more about God in my seven years in Africa than I have learned in the rest of my entire life." He says that in Africa, he learned a word: "Harumbai!" It means "all together!" He gave an example of how on a boat to cross the river, everyone had to pull a rope, from the oldest to the youngest. He emphasizes how if even one person took their hands off the rope and did not pull, everyone felt it. Each time they would pull on the rope, they would intone together: "Harumbai! Harumbai!" All together!

Okay, he has my attention now. I find that I am hungry for what he is going to offer. In the church where he was serving, he talked about five and six hour long services which were typical. People walked for miles along the dusty roads from small villages to what was surely the central event of their week. One day, he had prayed particularly fervently to God to show His face to him, something he had yearned for all his life. I sensed it was one of those prayers like I had prayed this morning, where you just turn to God like you would anyone you love, with simplicity and longing, faith and hope and you ask for your daily bread, knowing that it is God who can give it. If it is God's will, He will. No pretense. No posturing. Just "Ask and it shall be given thee" purely for love.

On this particular day, he had prayed that prayer, but even so, the five hour long services were sometimes too much for him. He said that he had taken to keeping a John Grisham novel hidden inside his prayer book. He would read at times, as the local African pastor was celebrating with the people, dancing and singing and calling out "Harumbai!" as he held up the folded bills of money that people were bringing and pressing into his hands with great joy.

He demonstrated the movements of the people and surprised me yet again by how agile he was and how in command of his audience. His body moved like some of the old aikidoists I knew, with a strong *Hara*[1] hidden in his well-developed paunch. When he made the outland-

---

[1] *Hara* is the Japanese word for the point just below the navel which is the center of balance of the human body, important to all martial arts. Cf. K. Durckheim, *The Vital Center of Man*. (England: Unwin Paperbacks, 1988) for a fascinating account. In Greek, κοιλίας is related to this. In Jn. 7:38, Jesus says of those who have faith in him, out of their κοιλίας (belly, womb, heart, innermost part) shall flow rivers of living water. The *heart* is not to be confused with feelings, but is related to the presence of a person that arises when the intelligence of awareness is united with the vitality of the bodily organism that becomes responsive to the action of Grace. Then the 'heart' experiences a sense of relatedness to all things that is otherwise not possible.

ish remark that surely this audience was familiar with becoming so caught up in the spirit that they danced during their liturgies, there was quiet mocking laughter. Appreciative, but also perhaps with dim awareness, like myself, that something might be missing. Privileged, comfortable, well-scripted lives often lack the freedom for that kind of spontaneous ebullient sense of community and joy that is given in greater quantities to the poor in spirit who may have next to nothing to make them comfortable in worldly ways, but who know something about celebrating together and sharing something intangible that the well-off hunger and thirst for without realizing it cannot be found by further acquisition. Or by seeking first to protect my self-image over relishing the experience of immersion in the moment.

He said that he had noticed that when someone handed the pastor a small amount, there was no "Harumbai!" He would just say "Thank you" quietly and place the money in the offering plate. So much for idealizing anyone. The same old passions infect the entire planet.

On this particular day, in the midst of the celebration with some 1,200 people packed in the church having walked miles and miles on foot to be there as they did every week, he heard an odd and strikingly unpleasant noise—CLANK! CLANK! of metal scraping against cement. As he was wondering what could be making this strange sound, slowly the sea of people in the church parted and silence amplified the messenger's arrival. CLANK! CLANK!

A small woman with hands and feet missing and the nubs of her limbs stuffed in tin cans, was crawling on all fours, straight down the middle of the church. She had a coin in her mouth, clenched between her teeth. The preacher reached out to take it, but she refused, insisting on dropping it into the plate herself.

It was a tiny coin worth less than an American penny, and as she bowed her head, it fell from her lips straight into God's hand where it was immediately felt by Stephen the Pharisee whose heart was undone at that moment along with most of the rest of those in the room who recognized truth and love when they witnessed it.

The priest said, "At that moment, my prayer was answered, and I knew I was looking at the face of God."

So *this* is what is meant by "Give us this day our daily bread." God is the giver. I am the beggar. The line of God's provision of me before I even realized what was happening began to coalesce and I realized that I too had seen the face of God today several times *and I had not even noticed.*

I had been given my daily bread by God from the hands of one whom I thought I was going to comfort with my presence and from another whom I had inwardly judged as inadequate to do so. Through these gifts, God showed me quietly and gently without crushing me, "Stephen, you pray to see Me and know Me and I am glad for this. I want to show Myself to you, but from the time you came into this room all you have done is sit above all the people, counting the coins of your self-righteousness, stroking your ego for your pitiful little offering of a fast while you withhold the greater fast that leads to humility, mercy, forgiveness, patience and love. Your whole thought process is 'holier than thou'—albeit in subtle, rarely noticeable ways. You judged all the people here, including the preacher, out of pride and greed and envy and then had the naïveté and temerity to call what you were doing 'spiritual.' The problem with you is that you ask to see Me, and then when I come, you are so busy looking for Me in other places and in other faces than those around you, that I cannot feed you. I cannot give you the daily bread for your *being*, because you are not aware of your deep *hunger* and your *need*. You are already so full from eating food which does not make for eternal life, satisfying your individual ego with knowledge that you lack an appetite for *Me*. There is no way of receiving the daily *being* bread that I give except "all together" realizing that *all* are equally as needy, from the oldest to the youngest, the wealthiest to the poorest, the healthiest to the sickest, the most religious to the least of all. *All* are My children. All together I save the world. It is you who refuse My table when you separate yourself from the rest. I invite all to the feast. It is you who refuse to enter in because I do not meet your standards and you cannot get through the crowded celebrations of your own self-righteousness in order to be simply the unique being I created you to be along with all the rest."

Following the prince of monologue and illusions, eating his devil's food of vainglory and self-righteousness, my heart is revealed to be far uglier and unkempt than any I would judge as outcast and far more privileged and above it all than any who might seem separated from the rest of humanity because of my own projections. It is I who am revealed as surviving only by the oxygen tank of God's breath and the grace and forgiveness of His fellow servants. Yes, Lord, I am hungry! I need You—in all Your ten thousand forms.

I went back the next week and sat beside Miss C. I learned she was moving in a week to a place nearer her son. I am glad for her. We prayed the Lord's Prayer all together, and out of the corner of my eye, I saw her face turned up to heaven with fervent intensity offering each word of the prayer as though it could be her last.

She had not offered me soup this time. But as I was standing up to leave after the dinner and talk, as if any doubt remained in my mind regarding the supernatural commingling with the ordinary the previous week, she abruptly turned around and looked at me directly, fixing her gaze on me. In that same loud and insistent voice, she spoke what could only be a prophetic word straight from God's lips to my heart, "Even if you don't like it, you are my brother. Jesus said so!" O Lord, Your flaming darts that wound the heart are more cleansing than a Lenten fast. Your bitter pill is the sweetest dessert. Your painful sword of truth cuts the heart only in order to heal it, turning cold stone back into flesh and uniting us with all life. Harumbai!

QUESTIONS FOR DISCUSSION

1. How am I a blind guide to colleagues, friends, and family without realizing it? What can I do to become more humble and self aware?

2. When in my life have I become the guest and my guest become the host at the table of God when least expected? How did it affect me?

3. How do self-love and secret judgments separate me from the people in my life making it hard for me to gratefully receive the gifts they have to offer in ordinary ways daily?

Rose of Sharing

Without faith that we will be understood somehow, sometime, by somebody, we would not speak at all. Or if we did,
it would be babble. And babble, as Dostoevsky shows in his
short story, 'Bobok,'is the language of the dead.

Mikhail Bakhtin

A QUICK GLANCE AS I BOARDED THE DC
metro for center city revealed a homeless woman with
soot-marked face beneath a mop of scraggly unkempt
hair, her arm cradling a bulging grimy bag with one long
stemmed rose sticking out of the side. A kind of pregnant
emptiness separated her from the frozen expressions of
the rest of the motionless commuters. It could have been a
wax museum. Nothing filled the spaces between the people except emotional emptiness and the roar of the train.

Several seats were open, but I found myself sitting
directly opposite her without the intention of doing anything in particular, just being *present*. She was missing a
few teeth, and the holes in her mouth made room for a
couple others to emerge at various angles. In the seat adjacent and facing her, an elegantly dressed, finely sculpt-
ed woman sat unmoving against the back of the seat with

Edited from an article first published in *Journeys*, AAPC, 2010,
vol. 12(1).

her legs crossed. Her whole body seemed as limp and forlorn as her face, gazing out the window and fixed on something within. Others had that deliberate "I'm not here" look of anonymous urban commuters or they were deeply buried in a book or newspaper.

After a few moments, somewhat shyly and hesitantly, the woman pulled out of her bag a huge harmonica at least a foot long and several inches thick. I had never seen such a monstrosity before. My interest warmed as she played, and I became fascinated by what appeared to be her decision-making process. She would put the harmonica away and then after a minute or so pull it out again and play another tune, though heads remained oblivious. This went on several times. What prompted her to begin to play just now? And for what purpose? Why did she hesitate ever so slightly and then try again? After a while, I began to feel as though no amount of attention would ever be enough to fill the black hole whose gravitational pull was beginning to make me anxious. The watcher was being watched. This was not dialogue, but a monologue, a performance designed to keep me—the generic 'other'— interested in her. But why? And what was the source of its pull on me?

I feared being sucked down into the vortex of hell this woman represented; the endless sea of human need and longing, torn between the impulse to give my lifeblood for one suffering the stinging rebuke of quarantine of her humanity by public invisibility resulting from the leprosy of homelessness, poverty, loss and trauma, rendering her untouchable as *other* and another impulse to separate my attention in order to save me from being consumed. But it came at the price of guilty acceptance of a secret consolation, feeling that I was somehow different; I wasn't *that* other...

What about my need and the invisibility of my own real presence which hides an acute awareness of God's absence? From there arises the longing for attention that is part of that distinct and essential life-giving *presence* beyond human comprehension at the heart of every true encounter with someone not of my own creating; someone who is *other* than myself which assures me that I do in fact exist. Is my monologue designed to attract attention any different than hers? My old seminary professor, Bruce Metzger, once said, "We will never know the degree to which Jesus was tested, because at some point, we always give in. He never did." How far will I go to meet others in the private hell of their abandonment by humanity which calls into question my own?

I turned slightly and felt my eyes glaze over along with the others, indicating I was withdrawing from the shared space between us and expected to be left alone, to retreat within myself as anonymous John Q. Public citizen. It was a subtle but definite shift. I was joining the crowd who was leaving this woman in the ditch of her miserable too-needy *otherness* on my way to the sanctuary of inner self-calming amidst the reflections in the mirrors that decorate the walls of the church of my own creation. Muttering under her breath to no one in particular, I heard, "He's tired of it already." How could it have been a monologue if she was noticing *me and ascertaining my own inner state out of the humility of her own soul*?

These words pierced my heart, opening up a different quality of space between us into which the blood of Grace and the fresh water of repentance flowed bringing me to my senses again. This woman, who, in spite of my attention and interest, had up until this point remained anonymous to me the practiced 'helper,' suddenly became *personal*. I recognized the pain of that loneliness and the conspicuous invisibility of being all too visible. Projecting shameful self-doubt onto others and then thinking that they felt this about me, I have refueled my secret misery in the depths of my hidden heart on far too many occasions. Now we were both human, sharing one pain, one life, drinking from one cup, hoping for the same nourishment of being visible and potentially beloved to someone, if only for a moment. I was her and she was me. And yet we were each very different. The space between us held the key to something vitally needed by one another. What to do?

We started a conversation. The first thing I discovered is that she was very much alive in her world. I learned she had once been a Gospel singer in a church choir and had taught herself to play the harmonica without any training. Vestiges of my outwardly concealed but inwardly maintained sense of superiority constructed out of the bric-a-brac of class, education, clothing, cleanliness, health, religion, having a job, a home, a family and anything else my inner press secretary can find to build up the portfolio of my manmade self to present the case for my worthiness to be noticed and loved, gave way to the possibility of dialogue between two souls sharing one commonwealth. The armor and privilege of spiritual capitalism gave way for a few seconds, allowing the call and response of a real meeting. We were both hungry for something that Mammon denies each of us, albeit in different ways.

Suddenly with renewed vigor, she announced she was going to play a Russian song that she had learned in her travels, deepening the mystery now collecting about her. Other faces had brightened with interest and surprise listening to our conversation, except for the well-dressed, sad-looking woman who continued to look away with an expression more of quiet pain than of disinterest. Even so, the wax had melted and the emptiness in between now contained something ineffable which arises "wherever two or more are gathered..." in such a way as to reveal our common origins and the shared blessing of our diversity.

Gratefully and without hesitation, I pulled out a ten dollar bill and gave it to her and then another person did the same. And another and then others started passing them on from the end of the car as though we had come to the conclusion of the sermon and the offering was being received. Only now the expression on the faces of the people resembled less the routine of "passing the plate" or the quick-glanced shameful toss of a charitable coin, than of the joy and delight that follow an exuberant encore at the theater.

Our guest of honor received all this without fanfare, stuffing the money into her socks. Then she announced, "I guess I had better get going before they come and kick me off." She pulled the long-stemmed red rose out of her bag without speaking and handed it to the sad-looking woman who took it in both her hands gently and lovingly without objection. The last of the sheep had been brought into the fold.

"Dasvidanya," I responded as she stepped off the train.

"Adios," she called out, leaving me wondering in the wake of her presence, if she really knew Russian and pondering One who *is* love and likes to appear unannounced in the unwelcome spaces between us bringing forth from the elements of our division the *manna* that unites us.

Questions for Discussion

1. What happened in the Washington DC Metro 'between' the people present there in the encounter? What do you think sharing the rose meant to the woman who received it and to the woman who gave it? Who has given you a rose when you most needed one in your life and it was least expected?

2. When have I experienced the pain of being regarded as so strangely "other" that I felt ostracized and made invisible to the people around me? How do I do this to others and why?

3. "A mirror that fails to reflect one who looks into it, becomes a thing to look at rather than into."[1] What kind of mirror am I to the people in my life, and who is my most accurate mirror?

---

[1] I believe this is a quote attributed to D. W. Winnicott.

Pascha in July

My food is to do the will of the one who sent Me.

Jesus

THE OLD MONKS SAY, "PRAYER BEGINS WITH remembrance of death."

One hot summer during a senior high youth mission trip to Washington, DC, we visited a shelter for the homeless. Several clear plexiglass boxes resting on the mantel piece of the Community for Creative Non-Violence were filled with dry white flakes, the relics of cremated homeless persons unknown to all but the staff who had known and cared for them. These elemental remains continued to inspire compassion and dedication in the hearts of those fighting burnout as they labored on behalf of the abandoned living remains of throngs of people circulating beneath the social radar in that limbo of invisible poverty lining the streets and back alleyways of our Capital.

As I sat in their communal living room before these unknown pilgrims listening to their stories, a heartfelt

Edited from article first published in *Columbus Ledger/Enquirer* in the Health Advantage supplement, Dec. 18, 1996.

shiver yanked me back to a time when similar silent cries rang out to me in Rome, Italy, from inside the "Church of the Bones." Fossilized chandeliers hung from the ceilings and walls covered with centuries-old relics of Christ's pilgrims who had lived out their lives in anonymity with intention and devotion in the adjacent monastery attached to the church. Human skeletal remains had been fitted with candles, adorning nearly every part of the interior, providing the only light. We were Jonahs, walking through the dank maw of a great Leviathan called mortality while eternity gathered in our hearts through remembrance of death. It was rendered almost visible by the contrasting musty cool draft wafting through the corridors like a wraith, clinging to the ribs of fellow sojourners drawn up out of the dust and fashioned into a sacred image by a living Breath.

Suddenly, it becomes clear. We are moving only for a brief moment, through days and years, down the long corridor of our lives through the family of humankind, oblivious to the fact that the earth, so beautifully adorned, is itself a Church of the Bones. We are each divinely inspired rebel priests in the belly of a great beast, whether knowingly or not, in one way or another, pondering the circumstances of our flight through the stars from God's loving embrace. Just beyond the film of our certainties are trembling birth pangs of some kind of spiritual quickening about to catch us unawares and plunge us willy-nilly through the jaws of death into the presence of our Creator, posed as a question to our own hearts. Here the pure light of Love and Truth will reveal us to ourselves and each other face to face without compromise or excuse.

Such a moment comes for us after several days of harvesting edible remains from the garbage of local restaurants and preparing food for the hungry of Washington's invisible back alleys. After walking the streets and talking with the invisible people of God's hidden Kingdom in their tattered, sweat starched rags, handing out second-hand clothes to the threadbare and unclean, we gather in a circle around a single loaf of bread and a cup filled with the blood of crushed grapes.

Silence is thick and deep, a rarity for teenagers ever on the move in pursuit of a new sensation, convinced they are already immortal. In this silence, God's ancient invitation to the great banquet of Life, "This is My body and blood which are given for you," rings like a bell in empty space. Spiritual resonance sounding in the heart shows forth in each attentive face. Without a single visible change, the veil of time is peeled back. Everyone is in awe of what God has done and what God is doing in our midst, "for as you have done unto those who appear least likely ... you have done unto Me."[1]

St. Basil expanded on the meaning of the Lord's words. "The bread you do not use is the bread of the hungry. The garment hanging in your wardrobe is the garment of the person who is naked. The shoes you do not wear are the shoes of the one who is barefoot. The money

---

[1] Mt. 25:40.

you keep locked away is the money of the poor. The acts of charity you do not perform are the injustices you commit." We thought we had come to Washington to feed the hungry only to discover that it is we ourselves who are fed by the ones asking us for bread and a drink of water. We have been entertaining angels unawares.

Suddenly, it is Pascha in July.

Questions for Discussion

1. When have I been most aware that I will die and that my life and the life of all those around me is total gift? What does awareness of mortality in this way make possible? What keeps me from seeking to be aware of this in my daily life more often?

2. How many pairs of shoes are in my closet? Pants? Shirts? Dresses? Televisions? What effect do many possessions have on rendering my heart unselfish and ready to share with Christ? Do I become less greedy the more I have?

3. When have I met and served persons whose poverty and need have revealed my spiritual poverty and the hunger and thirst hidden behind all my obvious satisfactions and privilege? What changes did I make as a result of this?

Good Enough

A child cannot be raised to be loving—neither by being beaten nor by well-meaning words; no reprimands, sermons, explanations, good examples, threats, or prohibitions can make a child capable of love. A child who is preached to learns only to preach and a child who is beaten learns to beat others. A person can be raised to be a good citizen, a brave soldier, a devout Jew, Catholic, Protestant, or atheist, even to be a devout psychoanalyst, but not to be a vital and free human being. And only vitality and freedom, not the compulsions of child-rearing, open the wellsprings of a genuine capacity to love.

Alice Miller

ONE EVENING I STARTED SKETCHING A PORtrait of my six-year-old stepdaughter Ami. She noticed what I was doing and came over and stood quietly beside me for the longest time as I drew. It tickled me that the little spark plug could stand stock-still for so long. She was already swinging a scarf around her and dancing like Carmen to Latino rhythms when she was four. It was one more way that her spontaneity and intense concentration in areas of her interest intrigued me. When I was finished, she looked at it excitedly and chirped in her staccato drill sergeant's voice, "Let's frame it!"

Edited from original first published in *The Pastoral Forum*, vol. 15(1), Columbus, GA: Pastoral Institute, Inc. (1998), pp. 6–7.

Who of us does not appreciate being carefully noticed by another and have that person seek to describe accurately the unique likeness in which we are made?

I told her after I had finished, "It's not good enough. We'll do another one sometime."

Her slumped shoulders showed she was immediately crestfallen. "I'm not good enough?" she questioned.

I had not said she was not good enough. It was my drawing that I did not hold in very high esteem. *It* was not good enough. It did not correspond sufficiently to her likeness I judged. It was imperfect, like the one who drew it. Did she not understand that? A twinge of regret flickered in my stomach.

"No, *you're* good enough, but this picture isn't. We'll do another one someday." She was thrilled with this distinction, and Claudia told me later that she had run upstairs with the drawing, burst into our bedroom and exclaimed, "I'm good enough, but this isn't! And we're going to frame it!" She had gotten the scissors and cut it out around the edges.

I never got a chance to draw a better picture because Ami was run over the following afternoon by a man in a pick-up truck and died twenty-four hours later with massive head injuries and a broken neck. It was the only picture I ever drew of her.

By her bedside in the hospital during the 24 hours that she lived, as I was quietly praying, I remembered the drawing and promised silently that I would frame it. It now hangs in my office lacquered onto a piece of wood—

my first icon. Since Ami was not baptized at the time, I found comfort in St. Hippolytus' words that unbaptized children who are killed are baptized in their own blood. The words "Good Enough" are inscribed beneath her picture to remind me of a choice that we must make over and over in life in order to prevent the spread of a disease that underlies much of the violence and hatred in the world: the disease of unbelovedness. And to help me remember that every person is a unique icon; every moment is precious and not to be wasted as inferior to the next, regardless of how imperfect I may judge it to be. It is in the present that we encounter *presence* which renders all things new.

This is especially true when it comes to our relationship with children. Infants fail to thrive and sometimes die when they are not held and cherished, even though they are properly clothed and fed. The younger they are, the less likely they are to distinguish our disappointments in ourselves from a disappointment with them. Belovedness is essential nourishment to the human soul and this remains true our whole lives. When it is missing, violence emerges, both with the mind and body, in the form of various diseases and higher mortality rates as well as with betrayal and addiction within our families and communities.

In the Genesis account, loss of belovedness is evidenced by the first human couple, Adam and Eve, who hide in shame from each other and from God as soon as they stop privileging the joy and gratefulness of dialogue with God in the immediacy of presence and replace it with monologue. Clinging to knowledge acquired in the past blocks access to relationship. On my own compared to God, I do not look so good. I begin to hide from the projections I make onto God and seek myself in images of perfection. Spiritual beguilement is a function of refusing God's grace while trying to clothe one's nothingness in enough illusory skins as to ultimately render an image that is good enough to ensure acceptance by the Lord not by grace, but by merit. It is an eternal trap. Comparing pictures and adjusting our imaginary tiaras becomes more vital than living life. The past begins to suffocate us. Once this disease of self-preoccupation broke out, it spread like fire. One of Adam and Eve's children murdered his brother out of envy and jealousy simply because, by comparison, in the isolation of his spiritual madness, he imagined God liked his brother better. He could not bear the pain.

Human response to the loss of belovedness has given birth to a wave of violence which has continued bearing fruit throughout ensuing millennia. We learn to notice what is not yet, more so than value what is. My professor of psychopathology told us a story from her childhood that I have never forgotten. "When I was 12, I wanted to surprise my father. I worked all day to plant 12 apple trees he'd recently bought, but I didn't quite make it before I was exhausted. When my father came into the yard that afternoon, the first thing out of his mouth was, "What happened to the 12th one?" It was so typical of him."

Not good enough. It is an existential virus which eats away our soulfulness, leaving us vulnerable to all sorts of mental illnesses, inciting forms of one-upsmanship to the point of denying the value and right to exist of others who are different from us. Unbelovedness is the root of a spiritual cancer against which we all need inoculation. Newborn babies seem perfect initially, miracles of life received with wonder like a visitor from another galaxy. Their vulnerability can move mountains and a single smile unclench the hardest heart.

Then slowly as they grow, parents discover more and more things they want to improve. With every exhortation to become better can come the implicit message, *You're not good enough* as you are. Another aspect of the problem is embedded in the culture at large in subtle forms of classism and racism. Minority children, and impoverished persons, even though loved by their families, still must find inoculation against covert forms of prejudice which pervade American culture that has not yet come to terms with the residuals of 250 years of conscious and unconscious attempts, by 'white' people to dehumanize and colonize their minds. We continue to confuse value with the power and privilege afforded by capital,[1] which remains enormously out of proportion along racial lines.

---

[1] The median net worth of whites in the U.S. in 2009 was twenty times greater than blacks, whose net worth dropped by one half in the previous three years compared to a drop of less than 1% for whites. In 2009, whites had a median net worth of $113,149, blacks $5,677, Hispanics $6,325. Reported in M. Jordan, "White-Minority Wealth Gulf Widens." *The Wall Street Journal. Economy.* Tuesday, July 26, 2011.

Growth and disease, like sin, are constantly occurring. Peace, to the extent that it can exist, cannot depend merely on arriving at perfection. This would make growth impossible. Is an apple imperfect when it is only a tiny green inedible ball on the branch? Is the smell of a gardenia perfect as it is or is it too sweet since it is not delicate like the rose? How about civilization? A planet? God does not expect a baby to write the Gettysburg address. A child with Down's syndrome is not faulted for not being able to do calculus. God's expectation of each and every part of creation and all of it together is that at any given moment, it be exactly what it is, on an infinite journey from glory to glory. We are not in the process of creating peace through arriving at perfection so much as removing the obstacles in our own hearts that distort and prevent our recognition of the unfolding goodness God has already invested in every part of creation and pours into us with each breath. What is it that blinds us to this so frequently? Why do we so fear being present to the mystery of the presence of the Other which is also what is of most interest to us?

Babies learn to walk without ever giving their spills and tumbles a second thought. The act of walking is intensely interesting to them. Tumbling to the ground is itself a discovery about the mystery of trying to stand and how that works. If babies reacted to their multiple failures in those first years of experimentation the way we learn to do later, but beating ourselves and one another up for not getting it perfectly right the first time, many, many babies would never learn to walk … or feed themselves … or speak. And if they did, they would think they deserved a special award or a trophy for it. The intrinsic value and worth of walking or eating or smelling a gardenia would be turned into an 'accomplishment' for which the child might seek some form of special credit. The action of living loses its intrinsic value. Trophies sit on a shelf and collect dust. If the living that the trophy symbolizes was not enjoyable, what is the point?

A 20-year study conducted by the American Psychological Association found that chronically drug-addicted persons already had in place the personality characteristics which made them vulnerable to drug addiction by age eight.[2] These children's parents had pressured them to improve and succeed, without enjoying their children. They failed to notice and appreciate what was worthwhile and valuable about them at each stage of their growth along the way. They had become a project more than a relationship. Consequently, the children did not have a sense of their own belovedness. Pressure to succeed was felt by these children like a hot sun beating down on them from which they could never find shade. Feeling deeply inadequate and unable to soothe the inner pressure constantly reminding them of this, drugs served as a welcome escape.

Another group of children turned to achievement in a driven, compulsive way. They appeared to have simi-

---

[2] J. Shedler and J. Block, "Adolescent Drug Use and Psychological Health: A Longitudinal Inquiry," *American Psychologist.* Vol. 45(5) (1990) 612–630.

lar psychological characteristics as the drug-addicted group — only achievement itself was their drug. In contrast to a third more psychologically healthy group of non-addicted persons, these two groups shared a sense of not being good enough, which disabled them from being able to take nourishment from appreciating life in the moment. The race to perfection (and avoiding the pain of failure and rejection) was what mattered most.

But this world will never be perfect on its own apart from διά-Λογος and neither will any of us. One of my mentors, Barry Estadt, used to say, "Christ did not come to change humanity but to embrace it." Paradoxically, in that embrace, we are changed precisely because we are loved as we are before our image has been fully restored. The medicine we receive from God is belovedness. It is a gift which comes through tears as we respond with gratitude and surprise to an embrace that is underserved and unexpected, like every aspect of the sheer thatness of each moment. As the philosopher Ludwig Wittgenstein wrote, "It is not *how* things are in the world that is mystical, but *that* it exists."[3]

God became Christ within Mary's womb and was laid in a manger as a sign to all that the Creator is already at peace with humanity not by our doing, but by the Lord's. This message and the subsequent message of the crucifixion and resurrection of the God-man Jesus is implicit and real in the communion offered to all through

---

[3] L. Wittgenstein, *Tractatus Logico-Philosophicus* (United States: Seven Treasures Publications, 2010), (6.44).

His Body and Blood. No psychological treatment in and of itself, and no human effort alone, is capable of bringing peace by convincing us of our worth. Why? Because only belovedness among all of us will enable the lamb and the lion within each of us to lie down together in harmony. Until this happens, we will continue the difficulties of our ancestors, projecting on to one another the imperfections we ourselves fear being aware of.

If this will not and can never be accomplished by human effort or design, how will it come about? God has drawn a picture of each of us in God's own image and given it to us from birth. It is this which calls us forward and consoles us in the worst of times that we too are "good enough" for God, even though what we have drawn with our lives is not. It is our very recognition of this and willingness to place our hope in God rather than ourselves, that is the most trustworthy sign that we have tasted God's love and found it good. With this, we might be able to say with joyful sorrow, "I'm not good enough, but God says *I am*. Gratefully I cling to God and place in Christ the hope that my likeness may bear His image for an eternity."

Questions for Discussion

1. In what ways in my life am I holding others at a distance until I am good enough? How do I judge others as not being good enough? What effect does this have on my life?

2. How does God see me? Who and when in my life has someone noticed me so carefully that I have felt beloved? What change resulted from this? Do I notice others in this way?

3. How do I celebrate and acknowledge the gift each one is? On a daily basis am I growing more toward being wondrously grateful or toward being critically hateful?

2:39 AM Gloria

Glory to God in the highest and on earth
peace and good will among humanity.
Luke 2:14

THE FIRST NINE MONTHS WERE A BREEZE,
filling the heart with sweet anticipation. In the last twelve
hours, I discover the shorter the wait, the longer it becomes. Slowly flesh softens to the divine hand. The cervix
expands like a rising sun and a new world appears on
the horizon for the first time. A 'crowning' is taking place
in the world through this portal linking uncreated Spirit
with the cosmos.

Every child is royalty; king and queen entering our
world in disguise from the lowliest place, hidden amidst
a sudden rush of interest in bodily processes. Enfleshed
soul is a Spirit-bearing pilgrim anticipating the birth
of flesh-bearing Spirit hidden within the mystery of a
second birth where soul-seed sheds the garment of skin
for a wedding garment not made with human hands in
order to enter the world a second time with the inheri-

Edited from an article first appearing as a personal reflection in
Journal of Pastoral Care & Counseling. Vol. 64(1) (2010).

tance of a new body united to a permanent unfading crown of glory.

Minutes pass in seconds and suddenly Elizabeth is here in our midst, all 8 lbs., 21.5 inches of her, trailing stardust in her wake. The Spirit has hovered over the waters for nine months and now takes her in arms, drawing life into lungs that begin to offer antiphonal response to the heart's insistent drumming, a reminder of the partnership between Creator and created— an internal Divine Liturgy holding everything together bringing lifeblood to all parts of the kingdom.

Well-formed ears, longggg fingers and big feet! So much detail. She looks like her great, great Granddaddy Trevathan. (Why is it every newborn seems like an old person in a fresh new body?) Blue eyes wide open, wander about, seeing without judgment, interested, humble, offering a special blessing to all upon whom they rest. She is finding a wondrous world and does not yet realize that she is wondrous to the world. This looking is what the saints hope to rediscover after a parabolic dive over a lifetime through the ecstasy and agony of the world trying not to lose sight of God's eyes looking through ours.

There is no cry until the nurse's needle pricks her foot drawing blood to tell the story of her vitality. It is in the blood. The story is in the blood. And written on the face with every movement. Now earth cries out. Prayer is this ache and ecstasy of heart beginning to fathom the cost of soul being thrust between Spirit and earth, not knowing to which we belong.

The power that this child's vulnerability brings to change the world is enormous. Every eye and look of soul is upon her entrance and remains present in wonder to every hair on her head, every turn of her face. Mother and father are speechless in new territory as momma's milk drops, beckoned by her newborn's vulnerability and Elizabeth takes her first mouthful. "I can feel it!" she says, discovering the life-giving mercy moving toward her child from within her own body. Daddy holds her swaddled in her blanket in his arms in quiet awe as she looks up at this being she is discovering who is her earthly father. Both embrace in the mystery of the silence, not yet realizing yet the mystery of the One who offers and the one who is offered who is between us in every place where we meet.

Yia Yia Claudia is smiling with joy and Papou is grateful to God. His heart bows and considers what gifts to bring this child, unsure any will be worthy of what she deserves. A grateful poverty for a moment renders the heart sensitive to an ancient revelation. He feels a little uncouth and coarse, like shepherds used to stony pastures and cold nights as the field of his soul is brightened and blessed just a little by the glow of this one who comes with the angels, visiting from another world with messages written all over her and whispers of joy ringing silently in every direction for those with ears to hear:

Glory, glory, glory to God in the highest and peace on earth among all of good will. For unto us a child is born who bears the image of our Savior in whom and through whom and for whom she is born this day in the city of Columbus, Georgia. Rejoice and be glad for she is destined for the great Temple of the Holy Spirit being built stone by living stone in the New Jerusalem of whom Christ is the cornerstone. The soft glow of joy from the Lamb of God who enlightens the world blends with the bright words of the angels whose voices mingle with the praise of humanity and seem to us like twinkling stars in the early morning sky. Rejoice on earth.

Shalom
Papou Stephen
December 20, 2007
Forefeast of the Nativity of Our Lord and Savior, Jesus Christ

Questions for Discussion

1. What do you recall of your first experience of looking into the eyes of a new-born child? What does the vulnerability of a child awaken in you?

2. Find a picture of yourself when you were three years old or younger. Be still and look gently at this "being" you once were. What do you feel? Where is that being now? Do you keep this part of you away from God? From others?

3. Imagine for a moment, being present at the birth of Christ, informed by the shepherds, of his birth and witnessing the Magi bowing before his manger. What happens in you as you behold this infant who is both human and God? What does he call forth from you? Do you share this kind of presence and attentiveness with the people in your life?

Snapping Turtle Lessons in Dialogue

The mark of contemporary man is that he really does not listen … I know people who are absorbed in 'social activity' and have never spoken from being to being with a fellow human being … Love without dialogue, without real outgoing to the other, reaching to the other, and companying with the other, the love remaining with itself — this is called Lucifer.

Martin Buber

ONE DAY I STOPPED THE CAR TO RENDER ASsistance to the largest snapping turtle I had ever seen: a veritable one-eyed giant at least two feet wide at the center. The kids and mom watched as dad had his first encounter of a close enough kind with this enormous and opaque alien presence, silent and still as a Dominican Friar as his radar took in the approaching menace now towering above him with unknown intent.

Grabbing him by the tail like my friend's neighbor, who says he nonchalantly drops them in a bag, clearly was not going to work with this behemoth. I reached out with both hands for the opposite sides of his armor. The sudden unceremonious *Harumph!* he gave me after he hunkered back into his shell and exploded like a jackhammer, his jaws flashing for a fraction of a second

Edited from an article first published in *Columbus Ledger/Enquirer in the Health Advantage* supplement, Feb. 1997.

more like a mako shark, let me know he was not exactly thrilled with my approach. My leg muscles spasmed, and the hairs on my neck stood up like straight pins as the adrenalin surged through me.

Now I was more excited than one should be when considering the best way to pick up a thirty pound razor-lipped, battle-hardened, special forces turtle on a singular mission to drag his armor plated self across the steaming July-heated asphalt. I reached for a stick, still thinking to pull him out of harm's way before some other unfeeling dinosaur on four wheels decided to nail him to the pavement just for the sheer entertainment of it. When his jaws clamped down, I read the message with my hand loud and clear. Had it been my finger, it would have had emergency room written all over it. I let go. He was not interested in my help. I do not think he even liked me! He certainly did not understand or care about my good intentions to render assistance.

With my newly acquired respect for the old mossy-back, I stood away and watched with awe as he continued his pilgrimage in his own good time. Humbly walking back to the car on rubber legs amidst the laughter and imitations of the whole scene by the kids, I was thinking to myself, "Just because you feel a strong desire to help someone doesn't mean they want you to or even that you will know how, even if you think you do."

Transformative encounter in its depths is always a meeting between strangers, evoking awareness of the unplumbed parts of ourselves. Even in familiar and trusting relationships, the fire that lights up the path of intimacy arises from sparks created by direct contact with the untrammeled bedrock of the soul beneath the familiar. Approaching the apophatic mystery of a person with the presumption of already knowing how to help someone simply on the basis of past history, or by virtue of having had many years of experience, ordination, a license or an advanced degree or whatever else is presumed to take the place of real presence, genuine loving interest and a willingness to be taught by the other, is a recipe for disaster.

Even a seemingly slow and plodding tortoise of a person, after downing enough of that potent elixir of unconfessed sins, losses, addictions, tragedies, and betrayals amassed over a lifetime, can temporarily morph into a mythical, fire-breathing, armor-plated snapdragon just waiting to take off a finger or spit out venom on anyone who dares to speak or listen in routine, clichéd ways indicating an unwillingness to risk a personal encounter. Such fire breathing is frequently in its depths a person's prayer to God who may seem just a little too frightening or a little too distant to be vulnerable enough to be affected by the slings and arrows of their outrageous misfortunes to even bother crying out. A person's spiritual pain may be rage at God for being such a cruel taskmaster. Or maybe it is the universe's indifference or any variety of the other false faces endlessly painted and projected onto God by our own self-judgments posing as knowledge about the other. The proverbial "log in my own eye" inevitably swings back as if from God, hitting me on the head until I give up and absent myself or reactively attack back. Persisting in faith with and for each other, means we are likely to catch a glimpse of parts of our own unexplored selves.

Paul Ricoeur observed somewhere, "The quickest way to the self is through the other." Jean Paul Sartre added, "The other is hell." The truth is that we become ourselves by our willingness to go through hell with and for the sake of the other. The risk of vulnerability and involvement are what together ignite vitality and passion. The price of admission is tolerating the anxiety and uncertainty along the way as you move off the edge of the map of the known world where fear of mythical sea monsters begins. Then like Jacob we wrestle face to face in the darkness with an unknown unconquerable alien presence receiving a blessing in the process. One approaches here a mysterious world encountered by the saints that dwells in the deeper fathoms of the human heart where, as St. Makarios the Great observed:

> There are dragons and there are lions; there are poisonous beasts and all the treasures of evil. And there are rough and uneven roads; there are precipices. But there is also God, also the angels, the life and the kingdom, the light and the Apostles, the treasures of grace — there are all things.[1]

---

[1] *Homilies* 43.7; trans. George Maloney, *Pseudo-Macarius: The Fifty Spiritual Homilies and the Great Letter* (New York: Paulist Press, 1992), 222.

To truly encounter another requires passion-bearing. One must be willing to be affected in his or her own self at the same depths and to the same degree as the person she or he encounters. This is why the Way of Christ is both desired and feared. Entering the silence and struggling in the darkness confronted by one's own and another's neglected and abandoned heart is at points like encountering a wild and wounded snapping turtle. God is not tame. Neither is the heart, nor the world present in the depths of our fallen human capacity for sin or that of our neighbor's, in spite of the pretty psychological clothing and custom designer-surgery garments of skin we wear to pretend otherwise.

To the degree that we actually reach out and touch the wounds we discover in ourselves and one another, it will indeed draw blood — if not from us, most certainly from God who is waiting there, to meet us in our private hells where we most fear to tread. In such encounters, the Spirit begins to speak in sighs too deep for words and the miracle of redemption begins.

QUESTIONS FOR DISCUSSION

1. What kind of listener am I? Do I seek to discover the world of another beyond my own projections? Am I more interested in being listened to than in listening? Do I always need agreement in order to remain in relationship with people because differences of viewpoints are threatening to me?

2. Who have been snapping turtles in my life and what have I learned from the encounters? What have I discovered from praying for my enemies? Do I seek to understand others on their own terms in their own context or do I assume they are just like mine?

3. When have I been willing to go to hell with and for the sake of another as a free gift of love? What blessing did I receive from this experience?

Antique Prayer

Constantly, each day, each hour, God is sending us people, circumstances, tasks, which should mark the beginning of our renewal; yet we pay them no attention, and thus continually we resist God's will for us. Indeed, how can God help us? Only by sending us in our daily life certain people, and certain coincidences of circumstance. If we accepted every hour of our life as the hour of God's will for us, as the decisive, most important, unique hour of our life — what sources of joy, love, strength, as yet hidden from us, would spring from the depths of our soul!

Alexander Elchaninov, *The Diary of a Russian Priest*

SOMETIMES MY OLD VAN SEEMS LIKE AN AN-tique. The right window does not work, and the air conditioner has a hole in it. The ceiling is hanging down in places like a Victorian curtain, and it burns more oil than gas. It seems much older than its 160,000 miles, wheezing with every turn of the odometer. It is only an eight-year-old model. When my grandfather was 96, we gave him a T-shirt that says, "Antique person," but he would not wear it. T-shirts are not his style. Suits are a sign of success.

In the last years of his life when he was telling stories, he would get confused and ask me if I remembered something that happened when he was 12 at the time.

Edited from article which first appeared in *The Pastoral Forum, Vol. 1.* (Columbus, GA: Pastoral Institute, Inc., 1998) pp. 7–8.

I like it when his love for me is such that at the feeling level in the immediacy of an exchange, he experiences me in his heart as an old home boy he knew when he got thrown from his pony, Roni, instead of his grandson for whom he was more like a father.

Old brains are a wondrous phenomenon. They do not work so well in places, like my van, but the driver inside is still precious and whole. Even though the connections of my grandfather's brain are crossed and worn in places, his soul shines through. I get glimpses of the impish, interested, adventure-seeking, sometimes brash, but genuinely beautiful human being he is — that boy that played with me when he was 9 and I was 43 ... or was it when he was 43 and I was only 2 ... In the midst of the joyful conversation, it really does not matter.

I think of an antique as something that is too precious for us to let wear out completely. Like the Velveteen rabbit, it should be worn enough to know it is loved a lot, but not so much it starts to seem uncared for. Prayer fits that definition. The more it is used, the more it is cherished and loved. Except that prayer does not wear out. It actually becomes more real by frequent use.

The Lord's Prayer is very, very old — ancient and so dearly loved by people all over the world that it is a priceless antique. It is wondrous that a few simple words would pass down intact through wars and pestilence, through tumults of migrating populations and be equally shared by billions without argument over squatter's right. It is free for the taking and yet imposes on those who truly love it, a price that can be paid only by selling everything you have to keep it. Imagine sending the message concerning something so precious in an envelope as fragile as words, which are so easily forgotten; yet they seem to remain forever.

Perhaps, it has to do with the fact that the Lord's Prayer survives only by love. I have a small cedar box at home full of treasures from my boyhood. I chuckle when I think of the things that I have kept: a giraffe's tooth, a Herb Score baseball card, an Apollo XIII badge from the original launch, and a few blue beads from the wristband that had my name on it as a newborn. They have remained safe while my treasured three-speed bicycle is long gone, along with my worn out Monopoly set, the USS Lady battleship that fired real plastic bullets and my silly putty and super ball. But I have kept that box with its treasures like I have kept the treasure of the Lord's Prayer in my heart since I first learned it as a child. Only I say the prayer a lot more frequently than I open the cedar box. I hope one day that the words will open my heart.

Professor Martin Buber tells my favorite story of the young rabbinical students in their first class. Their old rabbi instructed them first and foremost to "Hear, O Israel, the Lord Your God is One Lord and you shall love the Lord your God with all your heart and with all your mind and with all your strength and with all your soul. You shall write the words of this prayer on your hearts. Think of it when you get up first thing in the morning and when you take your shower. Do not forget it when you eat and when you walk to your class. Take it with you everywhere you go."

A young man raised his hand and asked, "Yo, rebbe, what good will it do to write the words on the heart? How about putting them inside the heart where they will do some good?"

The old man is pleased because he always gets this same question every year from his brightest and most eager young student in the beginning of their training. He seemed to ponder for a few moments and then responded slowly with a face full of gravity and kindness, "My son, no human being can put God's Word in the heart. So we make sure to write the words on our hearts and then, when the heart breaks, those words drop in."

The Lord's Prayer is written on many hearts like that, and it is a wonder to behold when it catches fire from the inner depths of a breaking heart. As pastor of a small country church where I knew the people well and loved them as my own family, I frequently had occasion to be with persons like my grandfather, very old in years, whose minds had frayed, whose bodies were almost completely worn out but who cried whenever they prayed. The fragile vessel that is home for the Holy Spirit of God had an antique finish. The brain that served as the safe deposit of precious keepsakes of a lifetime was fragile and insecure. So much forgotten, yet in those who had written the Lord's Prayer on their hearts from a former generation, something intangible and wondrous remained and it was humbling.

Margie was in her late eighties. I used to visit her at the nursing home regularly even though she did not speak. I would always find her sitting in the same place every day. Gradually, she had begun to scratch a hole in the skin on her head with a repetitive, seemingly mindless movement. She had once been the pianist in the church. Where had she gone? I would sit with her for a while and make one-sided conversation, feeling the silence at times threatening to weigh in on me with various kinds of doubts about what it was I was doing. Each time before I left, I would hold her hands and pray out loud the Lord's Prayer, and she would come to life. Her lips would barely move and from somewhere far aware from ordinary conversation that we could never seem to have, she prayed the words of the prayer out loud with me.

On my last visit not long before she died, she suddenly *appeared* and was *present*. She thanked me, with tears in her eyes, for coming to see her. Those words entered into my heart like sweet fire. James, the brother of our Lord who was convinced of his brother's Resurrection and who became the leader and first Bishop of the Church of Jerusalem in the days immediately after those wondrous events, nevertheless enjoined, "Pure religion undefiled is visiting the orphans and comforting the widows in their affliction."[1]

For a young pastor who thought that God's work might be done more effectively somewhere else with

---

[1] James 1:27.

folks who could talk intelligently about lofty theological ideas learned in seminary, the Truth of God's calling to His servant was delivered in a community where two were gathered in His name praying with one voice the prayer that Jesus taught those who loved Him. And then... when those words dropped in ... a third was present in our midst: διά-Λογος!

When Marion was on her death bed, I used to visit her even though close to the end she could not speak and did not appear to know what was going on around her. One day on my way back from the weekly Pastor's Bible Study, 50 miles away, I had a feeling that I should go immediately to the hospital to see her. No one was there when I entered. I walked in and sat down beside the bed. She was breathing in regular rhythmic gasps, and I sat silently in prayer quickened by the mystery of a soul so close to the other world that I could feel its presence. It is holy ground. Prayer has an intensity and greater clarity in the presence of death. I remember slowly praying out loud the words of the Lord's Prayer. As I finished, exactly at that moment, Marion's breath stopped and it did not return. Those words had dropped in again.

People who have grown up having learned to pray as these did in their youth present in therapy a capacity for growth and healing that exceeds that of those who have not. That is my experience. It is as if the seed of God's eternal life has a place to drop in the soil of a heart that has been prepared over time by the trials of life. Counselors talk about *good mothering* as a necessary ingredient for a healthy psyche. *Good praying* is equally important, and when it has been neglected, the road is more difficult, the options less. Still, with God all things are possible.

There have been enough moments like these for me to have no doubt of God's silent loving presence and the mysterious link of prayer to the invisible world of the Spirit. Yet, my human heart still waxes hot and cold, anxious and in between, at times confusing my mind left on its own without ground. Clearly, goodness and mercy and humble love are qualities of God's Holy Spirit, which we can participate in according to God's purposes, but we cannot make them happen. They are not *psychological* and subject to human will. God is not a cosmic bellhop. Prayer is not a *method* or a *tool* we can wield to get results, though they sometimes appear to come because God does indeed act. We can never be in charge regardless of what we think or feel or believe. Prayer is the language of love, a response of διά-Λογος crossing the chasm between this world and the next through the human heart.

Prayer is the blood of the soul and when it courses through the capillaries of our ordinary life, it brings us out of our daydreams, back to our senses refreshed by grace in a kind of breathing. When we offer a cup of water or fail to, we may still not realize what it is that we are doing and to whom. We are blinder and lamer than we realize. Nevertheless, we write the words on our hearts whatever we are doing, wherever we go, as often as we remember. Then, we simply live. And trust in God is there when the invisible cord snaps and we make an endless

fall back into His loving embrace. Surely, God hears His
Son praying with us in our sleep of death across the ages
of ages, and by the mystery of the Spirit, His words *Our
Father Who art in Heaven*...become ours and they will
remain forever.

QUESTIONS FOR DISCUSSION

1. Who or what did God place in my path this week through whom I have received unexpected spiritual refreshment through a personal encounter? Where and when did I became present to the mystery that *I am* and *Thou art*?

2. When have I experienced an inner 'nudge' that I listened to and acted on which led me to an encounter that revealed God's presence?

3. What action is within my power to make in order to experience who and what I encounter today as a gift from God? Am I renewing the inner act of attention to people and the world around me through the Thou of God in the present moment on a regular basis? (Or do I experience the present only filtered through the lenses of the past?) What keeps this from becoming my most important aim on a daily basis?

Gurus, Stars & Superheroes

> It is not that we find God and then realize that God created us from nothing.
>
> Rather, it is only in finding our own nothingness and embracing it that we realize God exists. For only an encounter with nothingness takes us far enough outside our world for us to realize that there is a giver of being who does not belong to it.
>
> *Jerome Miller*

THE RIPPLING MUSCLES OF THE MAN OF STEEL glistened from the front page of *Life* magazine's December 1992 issue devoted to "slain leaders." Familiar blue and red seamless Kryptonian clothes hung in shreds. Made from the Man of Steel's original swaddling clothes when he was but a babe thrust forth in a tiny capsule like Moses into the great river of stars before the destruction of his planet, they were supposed to be as invulnerable to the destructive forces of the universe as Superman himself. His bruised and battered corpse hung limp in the arms of his all-too-human lover, Lois Lane. Outraged, grief-stricken, despairing tears exploded from her eyes like artesian wells. It was not an altogether surprising choice for a culture that increasingly prefers the imaginary over the real and which expects human powers taken to the nth degree to save the universe.

Resemblance to Michelangelo's graceful and tragic Pietà was immediate and obvious. Yet the image failed to move. Why? Because we know that the ultimate crusader for truth, justice and the American Way is predestined for success along with Rambo, Dirty Harry, the Terminator and other Achilleans who personify the illusory triumph of good over human evil simply by means of raw power? Or is it because we knew resurrection would swiftly follow, predetermined by design in anticipation of increased sales of Superman #75, a prophecy which came to pass?

What do we want from the super men and women of our time who represent our collective daydreams? Rajneesh, Madonna, Michael Jordan, Christie Brinkley, Bill Gates and Lady Gaga ... to name a few of the many varieties available, who with a touch of their hand, the flick of an eyebrow or the twist of a word, a jump shot, a bra or a million-dollar bill, can create tremors of ecstatic interest in devotees, momentarily saving us from our *ordinary* lives. But spiritual health is not simply a "good feeling," nor is it charisma, or special powers. It is not about becoming somebody.

I remember in my twenties, being in the audience at the guru Meher Baba's Oceanside retreat at Myrtle Beach, South Carolina, when his secretary, Adi, had come from India for a visit to console and inspire the remaining "Baba lovers" following the Master's death. In the gentle lilting cadence of his melodious Indian accent, he related the seeming highpoint of his talk, "Baba made me so high. I was sooo high. He made me soooo high." That is about all I remember from his talk, other than impressions of the rapt attention of the blue-jean and sari-clad communal audience, holdouts from the psychedelic guru-hungry spiritual orphans of the sixties.

After some forty years in the spiritual desert of the world since that time, having looked for the promised land through a variety of methods, it is clear to me that getting high, acquiring special powers or amassing "security" through capital acquisition, or spiritual hedonism are not what real heroes do. Neither is spirituality about attaining greater self-esteem through psychological or transpersonal self-improvement. Without poverty of spirit, we do not care enough to receive life around us with love and mercy and interest. Without knowledge of human emptiness born out of being confronted by what we cannot overcome on our own, we cannot know God. St. Isaac the Syrian points out the blessing inherent in knowing one's own weakness "because this knowledge becomes the foundation, the root and the beginning of all goodness."[1]

Unlike the cameras of Hollywood which attempt to raise our human powers and passions to archetypal proportions where we are further enthralled and beguiled by the visage of humanity raised to mythological heights of the Olympian gods and goddesses (with our same unredeemed flaws written large!) it is only humility and poverty of spirit which enable us to *receive* the presence of the Divine *in and through the ordinary.* Even those who

---

[1] Cited by A. Vasileios, in *Abba Isaac the Syrian.* 2nd edition. (Montreal: Alexander Press, 1999), p. 26.

spend their lives in prayer, as the hesychastic[2] monastics, do so not as an escape from human life but in order to enter more deeply into it, weeping for the pain of the world. Embracing their own nothingness through grace-infused repentance, they become spiritual flutes played by the divine energies. One-pointedly set on encountering God, they are slowly released from their captivity to all other substitutes. Truly human persons are frequently invisible. They do not attract very much attention. Archimandrite Vasileios, Abbot of the Stavronikita Monastery on Mount Athos, in Greece, the center of Eastern Christian spirituality, describes the difference between personal charisma and the charisma of the Holy Spirit accruing to souls humbled by recognizing the emptiness of all worldly acclaim and valuing God's Grace above all.

> Great are not the noise-makers who raise themselves as spiritual leaders or prophets, to amaze and to asphyxiate the world. Great is the humble and "nonexistent," who have received the supplication of the Spirit and are the consolation of the world.

---

[2] Hesychasm comes for the Greek word ἡσυχία which carries the meaning of quiet, silence and stillness. Hesychasts are those whose love for God leads them into intentional inner stillness of prayer and watchfulness, living in silence where they seek to encounter God in every moment through continual repentance. For a good example, see Joseph of Vatopaidi, *Elder Joseph the Hesychast: Struggles, Experiences, Teachings (1898–1959)* (Mount Athos: Vatopaidi Monastery, 1999) and A. Sophrony. *St. Silouan the Athonite* (Crestwood, NY: St. Vladimir's Semianry Press, 1999).

Grace is enough for them. And this they emit perpetually with the radiance that endlessly feeds from the contrition of the heart and the feeling that they have polluted the land with their presence. Yet they themselves are a blessing for all creation while they live and though they may pass, because the Holy Spirit gives meaning and reason to their presence and absence. On the other hand, once you believe that you are something in virtue or knowledge, then you lose everything and you become polluted, regardless of whether you — or others — think that you are a model of virtue and the renewal of spiritual life. That which is possessed by the Saints is not human talents or qualities: wisdom, poetry or rhetoric. But all these they sanctified by offering them to God. And through them is manifested the Grace that comforts and deifies humanity.[3]

Souls on fire with the quest to become super men and women may even fail to notice and appreciate treasure in such ordinary vessels. It is our culture's incessant and infantile desire to withhold love until we find the perfect body, the perfect mind, the perfect mood, the perfect mate, or until we possess the perfect "me-ness" ... which renders us vulnerable to the same old seduction that began long ago in a Garden called Eden. To the degree

[3] From the book *Apolytikion*, translated from the Greek by John Sanidopoulos. Posted Sunday May 22, 2011, http://elgreca262. blogspot.com/2011/05/archimandrite-vasileios-of-iveron.html.

that we are all striving, in one way or another, to become something, we are missing out on the privilege of being nothing. Yet "it is the Father's good pleasure to give (us) the kingdom."[4] What is the blindness and grasping that leaves us in search of something that will make us worthy of what can only be given as gift? Like the first Apostles, "we do not understand about the loaves."[5] We still choke on the apple of self-sufficiency, a fatal mistake. The simple fact is God-esteem is infinitely more life-giving than self-esteem and infinitely rarer. The road of love begins where I end.

---

[4] Lk. 12:32.
[5] Mk. 6:52, Mt. 16:9.

Questions for Discussion

1. How do my life and the choices I make reveal that I value God-esteem over self-esteem? How was this in evidence in my life today?

2. How has my heart been open to the love of God and the gifts of other people today? Have I taken joy in other's joy and sorrow in other's sorrow? Have I noticed the hostile pleasures of jealousy, envy, resentment and unforgiveness prowling about in my mind waiting for a chance to leap into my heart and devour all my energy?

3. What person above all others in my life has been an icon revealing Christ to me? What qualities about him or her were most revealing in this way?

The Buggy Man's Spiritual Jazz

Of course, I am aware of individual sins of which I accuse myself, but I believe that they take up less room in my life. What I suffer from, and what I need and seek forgiveness for, are all the disastrous things that we, as a society, inflict today on the poorest of the poor and on our mother, the earth… Often the God of Christians is no more than a non-corporeal, heavenly being above and beyond history's victories and defeats and is experienced exclusively by individuals in connection with their individual fortunes.

Dorothee Soelle

GEORGE SMITH WAS KNOWN IN COLUMBUS, by those who did not really know him at all, as the "buggy man" after years of seeing him pushing his overflowing grocery cart along the sidewalk or lying slumped over it, covered in overcoats in the July heat. He had become a fixture in many people's busy lives — kind of a spiritual toll booth passed on the way to work and coming home again.

After he landed in the hospital, the local paper published an article about him because so many people missed seeing him on the streets. It turns out that in his younger days, he had been a musician, and it seems he still owned a house he did not live in. Long after he had

Edited from article published in *The Bridge* newsletter of the TMRC of the Pastoral Institute, April 2009.

stopped playing saxophone in local clubs with a group called Spot Rivers and the Nightingales, for unknown reasons he had taken a gig on the streets playing silent jazz that tugged hard at people's souls pulling in opposite directions — the kind of spiritual melody that makes a person feel love so deep down in the heart that you want to exchange your body with the first leper you meet and on the other hand you want to pass on by as if the person was invisible and already dead.

What is the source of this strange angelic power of otherness that crosses our familiar paths bringing us into confrontation with wild and sacred places that we so often and easily ignore? Wandering pilgrims who call no place home and have no names except the ones we give them in our efforts to tame their effect on us are the ones we want to contain. We put them in some kind of box that mutes the questions stirring in our hearts from having too close an encounter with one so totally other that it might shake up our comfortable world. We want them to accept a little food or a little do-gooding to release us from the pangs of conscience, that if given free reign, threatens to spread out beyond one homeless person to encompass other ills in our society — like our forgotten vets who at one time were estimated to make up about a third of the homeless men in America.[1] After they have done their killing for us, we are not willing to hear their stories and help them find their way back home into our

[1] According to the Veterans Administration, in December 2010, there were 9,000 homeless veterans from the OEF/OIF wars.

lives and their own. They are easier to ignore. Or those
with chronic mental illness who are forgotten and hidden
in broad daylight on the streets of our cities because we
cut the funding of the hospitals that cared for them.

We want to assuage the nagging, still, small voice[2]
deep within that asks why one out of thirty Americans
are or have at one time been in jail — more than five times
the number of any other nation on earth. Among these
are disproportionately represented the descendants of the
indigenous people and former slaves. Denial of America's
invisible pariahs is a part of our societal post-traumatic
spiritual disorder — a kind of collective dissociation[3] that
prevents us from healing the invisible wounds that the
buggy man bears for us. What his silent music stirs in us
might entail much more than singular acts of kindness.
Mahatma Ghandi refused to offer handouts to the poor.
Jesus wandered about Galilee homeless Himself, raising questions about the sincerity and depth of religious
forms and the presence of God's love, until governmental
and religious authorities felt threatened by His spiritual
jazz. Socrates suffered a similar fate for questioning what
people thought they already knew about life.

George Smith refused all handouts too. He was of-
fended by the action, and it showed on his face if you

---

[2] I Kings 19:12.
[3] Cf. S. Muse, "Post Traumatic Spiritual Disorder and the False
History Syndrome," in *When Hearts Become Flame: An Eastern
Orthodox Approach to the διά-Λογος of Pastoral Counseling* (Rollinsford, NH: Orthodox Research Institute, 2011) pp. 247–286.

approached him. By God's mysterious power at work in the faith of people's hearts, his was a prophetic voice and presence in Columbus, Georgia. Prophets of all ilks do not cotton to being toned down very easily, bought off, or co-opted into the mainstream so we can all go back to sleep in the warmth of our collective privilege—we Americans on whom, at last count, 32 times more resources of the world are lavished per capita, than all the rest. We are used to this. We expect this. We feel entitled to it. That is what having power and privilege do. The disparities between the elite and the rest have been increasingly unequal since the founding of our nation.

The "buggy man" challenges us to explain why someone has to push a loaded cart around, covered with layers and layers of unnecessary heavy clothes and even sleep standing up, holding on to his possessions. He is a Jeremiah lamenting his people's chains, going naked through the streets, and by his very actions and startling presence shedding the clothes of civility, thereby showing us our bare-naked spiritual slavery to the Emperor of Mammon and his minions.

It is Mammon who gives us our daily dose of over-consumption — all those things unnecessary for becoming fully human that keeps America and the global economy spinning like a top, driving up health care costs and necessitating Prozac prescriptions- creating a need for boredom-breaking computer games of greater and greater violence that all major health associations agree injure our children's psyches. Why do we ignore the danger of this insidious 'drug' which is even more serious to our society than those we spend billions trying to prevent coming across our borders? When our legislatures try to pass laws to protect our children from the plague of this violence and pornography, we appeal to free speech and unfettered capitalism as a greater good. Could it be that what so disturbs us, like the comic strip character Pogo, is that our eyes have beheld the buggy man pushing an overstuffed cart full of useless junk along the boulevard...and *he is us*?

George Smith is a modern-day specter of John the Baptist. We see him there on the edge of the wilderness looking out from the shadow of civilization as we drive our gas-guzzling greenhouse gasifiers back and forth to church every Sunday and to work every day, laboring increasingly longer hours in order to make more money to buy more things we don't really need and are unlikely to be able to lovingly care for. We see George and his buggy on the way back and forth in this maze and hear a voice crying out from the wilderness of our own hearts. It cries out for sobriety and a willingness to bear the tension inherent to the fact that Esau and Jacob, Hyde and Jekyll, the pauper and prince, Indian and American, Palestinian and Jew, and all the hidden segregated parts of our own souls and of our community cannot remain this way forever. As our vanishing indigenous peoples realize better than most, we are one flesh; we belong to one earth. President John F. Kennedy emphasized this in his strangely ignored "peace speech" — given at the commencement of

American University, June 10, 1963. "We all inhabit this small planet. We all breathe the same air. We all cherish our children's future. And we are all mortal."[4] It cannot be otherwise. We do not and cannot own the earth and life any more than we can or should own each other.

The farther we are from understanding this, the starker and more bloody will be the cut of our conscience awakened by the witness of these silent, spiritual musicians who, as the Holy Spirit, are "like the wind which goes where it will and you know the sound of it…but you do not really know where it comes from or where it goes."[5] So it is with George Smith, the saxophone-playing buggy man. You hear his melody and can't quite get the trill of its glissando out of your mind. Perhaps because the sound comes from the Holy Spirit and catches fire with the sparks arising in one's own heart which knows it is somehow connected with our Common Creator … a love supreme … and with every common human fate.

Play on brother. Play on!

---

[4] http://www.ratical.org/co-globalize/JFK061063.html reproduced from *John Fitzgerald Kennedy… As We Remember Him*, Columbia Records Legacy Collection Book, New York: Atheneum, 1965) pp. 192–195.
[5] Jn. 3:8.

QUESTIONS FOR DISCUSSION

1. When I am approached by someone begging on the street, what is my first reaction? Do I give in order to avoid an encounter or avoid a real encounter in order not to have to experience my conscience?

2. Are the poor and needy in our day different than those in Jesus' time? Do I pass judgment on the beggar? "He's probably just going to buy alcohol with it?" Have I noticed that I speak in cliché's when it comes to confronting the inequities in society? If so, what does this mean?

3. How would my thoughts, feelings, and behavior change if I realized that the homeless person and beggar I passed by offering nothing, was the Lord. How would I respond if he came after me and offered his life for mine? How and why do I ignore the depth of Christ's presence in the ordinary in life as often as I do?

Indian Givers and the Holy Trinity

The Arrowhead

The arrowhead,
which I found beside the river,
was glittering and pointed.
I picked it up, and said,
"Now, it's mine."
I thought of showing it to friends.
I thought of putting it — such an impos-
    ing trinket —
in a little box, on my desk.
Halfway home, past the cut fields,
the old ghost
stood under the hickories,
"I would rather drink the wind," he said.
"I would rather eat mud and die
than steal as you still steal,
than lie as you still lie."

Mary Oliver
Why I Wake Early (Boston: Beacon Press, 2003)

"INDIAN-GIVER" IS AN EXPRESSION WHICH IN its Americanized meaning has the ugly connotation that an Indian is one who takes back whatever gift he gives you. This view is rooted in a terrible misunderstanding (or disinformation) that reveals more about the underlying fears and cultural supremacy of the ones who disseminated it than the ones from whom it was taken.

Some years ago when my Lakota brother Canupa Gluha Mani (a.k.a. Duane Martin. Sr.)[1] was visiting us from South Dakota, I gave his son Duane, Jr., a prized Buck knife as gift. He placed it back in my hands and told me to return it to him. We did this three times. He said this is a sign among his Lakota people of extended family. Family is grown and sustained through love which gives away what one has for the sake of the welfare of everyone. Ohiyesa, (a.k.a. Charles Eastman, M.D.), another Lakota man raised as a traditional warrior until the age of 18 before attending Dartmouth College and completing his M.D. at Boston University, elaborates on how important unselfishness was among the traditional Lakota people he knew in the 1800's before white civilization began to interfere with it:

> It was our belief that the love of possessions is a weakness to be overcome. Its appeal is to the material part, and allowed its way it will in time disturb the spiritual balance of the man. Therefore the child must early learn the beauty of generosity. He is taught to give what he prizes most, and that he may taste the happiness of giving, he is made at an early

---

[1] He is the leader of the Cante Tinze or "Strong Heart" warrior society of the Lakota people whose name means "He who walks and protects the sacred pipe." Duane has been educated in white schools, after being raised fluent in his the native Lakota language, learning its traditional stories and keeping its traditional Way. He works to serve his people and keep the Traditional Lakota culture alive.

age the family almoner. If a child is inclined to be grasping or to cling to any of his little possessions, legends are related to him, telling of the contempt and disgrace falling upon the ungenerous and mean man...The Indian in his simplicity literally gives away all that he has, to relatives, to guests of another tribe or clan, but above all to the poor and the aged, from whom he can hope for no return.[2]

In the language of the Oglalla Lakota people, the word for white man is *wasichu* which means something like "the fat taker," or "he who takes the best part for himself." This represents a dishonorable and painful departure from the traditional Lakota way of life, the very opposite in fact, as it was the honor of the warrior who killed the buffalo, to offer the best pieces of meat to the other members of the tribe. As in any family, the strongest always take care of the weakest. This is in stark contrast to how the Lakota experienced white culture behaving, where the strongest took the best and kept it for himself.

"The human tragedy" according to Archimandrite Zacharias of Essex, a spiritual son of Elder Sophrony, "is that humanity lives and prays and speaks outside the heart."[3] In other words, we live without love. There is not

[2] M. Fitzgerald (Ed.), *Light on the Indian World: The Essential Writings of Charles Eastman (Ohiyesa)*. (Indiana: World Wisdom, Inc., 2002) p.26

[3] From a talk given in 2007 at the Antiochian clergy retreat in Wichita, Kansas.

life·to our actions, words and prayers, because love is what gives them life and love is kindled through the fire of Grace acting in the heart.

Once in Russia while visiting the Optina Monastery, several of us had the unexpected privilege of having a meeting with their renowned Staretz Ilia. When Matushka Evgenia took us to the refectory to get his blessing, the elder noticed us and asked us to wait for him. He gathered up some of the small loaves used as *antidoron* which had earlier been given out to the people who were packed like sardines in the church for the five-and-one-half-hour worship service. I noticed a thread of greed reaching up through me insidiously. Before long my inner press secretary was playing the strings of the harp of vainglory whose melody was meant to hypnotize me into the sleep of basking in a secret specialness that placed me above others. The thought of having been given this gift by the staretz increased vanity which further alienated me from the action of Grace in the heart. My mind began wrestling with whether to give the bread away immediately or to keep it for myself. The rationalization that I was saving it for my family at home won the day in helping me deceive myself that I was not simply responding to selfish greed and vainglory.

I, the *wasichu*, proved once again how easily I succumb to the disease of taking what God offers and keeping it for myself alone. When I got home, the bread had turned green with mold, ruined like the manna the Israelites had gathered against God's word, not trusting Him to care for them moment by moment as God had promised.

Because of my selfishness and self-centeredness, neither I nor my friends, nor my family benefitted from the Elder's gift. The wounding of this recognition was God's gift to me, showing me once again my sinfulness and how far I am from humility and real love which can be increased only by being given away.

When we love, the world appears as it truly is. *Being-in-love-in-relationship* sustains it. According to the opening words of the book of Genesis, "In the beginning" God said "Let us make humankind in *our* image, in *our* likeness."[4] This is an odd expression given the revelation that "The Lord Your God is One Lord..."[5] Later, after the birth, life, death and resurrected appearances of Jesus in the flesh to his disciples and others, the image of Father, Son and Holy Spirit comes more clearly into view, whose circular dance of eternal self-offering love is both communal and uniquely *personal*—one *essence* shared among three *persons*. God is *three* and God is *one*. How is this experienced?

Given the fact that the world's assets are gravitating upward into fewer and fewer hands, the spirit of worldliness or "taking the best for oneself" appears to be spreading at exponential rates. Now the top 200 richest people in the world have more than the combined assets of 41% of the world's population![6] The *wasichu* spirit of worldliness tempted Jesus on the mountain in the wilderness af-

---

[4] Gen. 1:26.

[5] Deut. 6:4.

[6] R. Inchausti, *Subversive Orthodoxy: Outlaws, Revolutionaries, and Other Christians in Disguise* (Michigan: Brazos Press, 2005) 86.

ter his baptism and continues to do so through each one of us. We struggle in our hearts how we shall respond to the gifts of God given freely to all. If "worldliness is the capacity to look past the unfair distribution of the world's wealth in order to affirm one's right to the spoils,"[7] godliness is the willingness to abandon that delusion and recognize that our lives only become our own when, like Jesus, they are given back to God for the life of the world.

According to the ancient Lakota way of life, gifts are given in order that all may have what is needed. In this way a gift that is offered by one may circulate through the others in the same generous spirit of sharing, eventually returning to the one who first gave it, making a full circle of selfless giving, breathing life throughout the entire community. Rather than having the selfish connotations white culture has given the term "Indian Giver," in actuality, the meaning is an accurate and beautiful description of the *perichoresis*[8] of love among the three persons of the Holy Trinity, capturing the very essence of the ideal Christian

---

[7] Ibid., p. 92.

[8] Perichoresis is constructed from the Greek words περί, "around" and χώρα for "space" used by St. Gregory of Nazianzus and others, to signify the mutual indwelling of the persons of the Father, Son and Holy Spirit. As this is explained by Jesus to the disciples in John 14–17, once the Holy Spirit is given to them, they will dwell in Him as He dwells in the Father and all will be perfectly one. Perichoresis refers to the mystery of the unity of the three distinct persons of the Trinity who reciprocally contain one another through the coinherence of their self-emptying love. "One permanently envelopes and is permanently enveloped by the other whom he yet envelopes." (Hilary of Poitiers, *Concerning the Trinity* 3:1).

community described by St. Luke in the *Acts of the Apostles* in which all the believers were of one heart and mind and they freely shared everything they had for the sake of all.[9] God the Father has given everything to the Son[10] and the Son gives Himself completely for the life of the world[11] Who is raised up through the Holy Spirit along with all who live in and through Him, in an endless circle of love.

In reality it appears that in many significant ways, the Lakota Indian people were closer to Christianity than the whites trying to convert them. As part of his work establishing the YMCA legacy, Dr. Eastman travelled all over the United States meeting with various Indian tribes. Observing the progress of Christian missions among the Indians, he began to reflect.

"I asked myself how it was that our simple lives were so imbued with the spirit of worship, while much church-going among white and nominally Christian Indians led often to such very small results. A new point of view came to me then and there. This latter was a machine-made religion. It was supported by money and more money could only be asked for on the showing made; therefore too many of the workers were after quantity rather than quality of religious experience."[12]

---

[9] Acts 4:32.
[10] Jn. 3:35.
[11] Jn. 6:51.
[12] M. Fitzgerald, p. 192.

He recalls the irony of some of the Indian's observations of white 'Christian' culture.

> "I remember one old battle-scarred warrior who sat among the young men got up and said, in substance: "Why, we have had this law you speak of for untold ages! We owned nothing, because everything is from Him. Food was free, land free as sunshine and rain. Who has changed all this? The white man; and yet he says he is a believer in God! He does not seem to inherit any of the traits of his Father, nor does he follow the example set by his brother Christ."[13]

Another said,

> "I have come to the conclusion that this Jesus was an Indian. He was opposed to material acquirement and to great possessions. He was inclined to peace. He was as unpractical as any Indian and set no price upon his labor of love. These are not the principles upon which the white man has founded his civilization. It is strange that he could not rise to these simple principles which were commonly observed among our people."[14]

An old chief named Little Fish said of President McKinley: "I never knew a white man show so much love for

---

[13] Ibid., pp. 192–193.
[14] Ibid., p. 193.

mother and wife. He has a bigger heart than most white men and this is unfortunate for him. The white man is a man of business, and has no use for a heart."[15]

> "I confess I have wondered much that Christianity is not practiced by the very people who vouch for that wonderful conception of exemplary living. It appears that they are anxious to pass on their religion to all races of men, but keep very little of it themselves. I have not yet seen the meek inherit the earth, or the peacemakers receive high honor."[16]

After a deeply multicultural experience and education in two vastly different worlds, having had many of these kinds of dialogues in his lifetime, near the end of his years, Ohiyesa/Eastman wrote what might be a fitting paradoxical epitaph worthy of pondering, in so much as it points us toward the one which Christ himself embraces in His two natures that reconcile the Spirit world and this one of earth and sky, river and ocean. It places our daily *being* bread of love at the center where it belongs, transforming commerce rather than becoming a slave to it.

> "I am an Indian; and while I have learned much from civilization, for which I am grateful, I have never lost my Indian sense of right and justice. I am for development and progress along social and

[15] Ibid., p. 196.
[16] Ibid., 202–203

spiritual lines, rather than those of commerce, na-
tionalism or material efficiency. Nevertheless, so
long as I live, I am an American."[17]

Life is meant for διά-Λογος between the uncreated and
created worlds, a communal liturgical dance and hymn of
praise in the form of continual self-offering through call
and response. Everything is εὐχαριστιακὴ ἀναφορά[18] (offering of thanksgiving) returned to the Giver, blessed,
divided and shared among all. When we pray "Thy will
be done on earth as it is in heaven" we are praying for a
world that is lived on earth the way the Holy Trinity lives
among themselves in heaven—as eternal *Indian givers.*

---

[17] Ibid., 203.

[18] The anaphora refers to the action of the priest in the Divine
Liturgy who offers up to God the chalice containing the bread
and wine which is received back as the Body and Blood of Christ
given for the life of the world. This action of freely referring the
created world back to the uncreated God in thanksgiving is continual prayer, the central act of the human person. It constitutes
the lifeblood of royal priesthood (I Peter 2:9).

QUESTIONS FOR DISCUSSION

1. What do you think of the Lakota Indian's perception that Jesus sounds more like an Indian than he does a white man?

2. In what areas of my life do I fail to be an Indian Giver? What am I attached to so much that I do not want to share it with others? How does this affect my relationship with others, with myself and with God?

3. If someone stole something from me, would I ever consider it not stolen, regardless of how much time had passed? Does the behavior of our civilization demonstrate that we are Indian givers with all that we have control of? Why or why not? Do you judge the progress of civilization based on its technology and material assets or its conscience and ability to care for all of its members?

Settling the Score
a Different Way

Enemies have taught me to know what hardly anyone knows, that a person has no enemies in the world except himself. One hates his enemies only when he fails to realize that they are not enemies, but cruel friends. It is truly difficult for me to say who has done me more good and who has done me more evil in the world: friends or enemies. Therefore bless, O Lord, both my friends and my enemies.

St. Nikolai Velimirovic

A person is humble when he knows that his very being is on loan to him.

St. Maximos the Confessor

LAST NIGHT A CHILDHOOD FRIEND APPEARED in my dream as a member of a visiting team of scientists come to investigate a beautiful, intuitive and carefree animal on loan to me...

If pocket calculators and laptops had been invented back then, Gary would have had one. In High school he excelled in chemistry and physics, but by then we'd already lost touch. Years before in the halcyon days of our childhoods, we had built forts together, played chicken on bicycles, and spent hours re-inventing the nooks and

Edited from an article first published in *Columbus Ledger/Enquirer Health Advantage Supplement* March, 1998.

crannies of his big basement for our covert ops. We played ping-pong, climbed trees and had wars with acorns and ripe persimmon grenades. On rainy days we puttered with old batteries and tiny motors imagining ourselves scientists. It was all fun, but thirty-five or so years later, I remembered him best as the boy whose tooth I knocked out with a rock.

Come to think of it, my memories of friendship with him disappear shortly after his quiet, sweet mother's explosive phone call to our house after she discovered the chip on his tooth and the little hoodlum who was responsible for it! Now here he was come to me in my dream as a "visiting scientist." to inspect the *carefree, playful creature on loan to me*. Hmmm.

In those magic Speilbergian days shortly before the "incident," Gary had been tormenting me along with some other boys under his leadership. I was confined to my backyard as punishment for a deed I no longer recall. There is something odd about remembering the punishment more than the crime. At least with confession and grace we may remember the sin but the intimate restoration is even more precious. Reconciliation is swift and clean and leaves no residue of vengeance or shame to further disable the heart. Light chases the darkness away. Envy is an insidious passion and easily kindles into revenge under the right conditions. The hostility associated with these cold, quiet flames are among the most dangerous emotions known to human physiology; perhaps to the soul as well. Forgiveness, not forgetfulness, is the only antidote.

In spite of our friendship, envy of Gary was never far away. He was a year older than me and he had a father. He was the first boy in the neighborhood to own a three-speed bicycle. When McDonald's came to town he was the first one to boast of having had a McDonald's hamburger. The odd confusion I felt after the insipid blah of eating my first Mcburger has never left me. A little ketchup and mustard smeared on a white bun with a thin sliver of something in the middle that was difficult to describe as meat didn't come close to the succulence of thick homemade ground beef burgers cooked by my grandfather on the outdoor grill loaded with onions and fresh tomatoes. And yet...there was this strange magical attraction to McDonalds...and the fact that Gary got there first.

The power of revenge harbored out of awareness waiting for a time to be born happened like this. Gary and some of our mutual friends had broken off long sharp thorns from a honey locust tree and they were coming in and out of my yard threatening me with them like adventurous swordsmen. All I had was a leaf from one of our Holly bushes, which I was well aware paled by comparison. I was interested and caught up in the adventure, but also a little humiliated because I'd never thought of co-opting a locust thorn in the service of childhood bravado and temporary knighthood. Surely that's what real boys did ... I was confined and they were free. I did not realize then, how the gaping wound of the loss of my father had left a well of grief in me covered over by a sense of shame and unworthiness that seemed to attach itself to certain things in my life as if reminding me of a far-away, dimly forgotten injury it was necessary to protect myself from at all costs. By comparison these boys now seemed strong and powerful and somehow preferred. Cain was rising up within me from outside my awareness, resenting my brother Abel, and waiting for an opportune moment...

Some days later, the unholy leaven of comparing myself to others and failing to measure up, developed into ripe fruit. Gary had been watering that seed a little too much one day by riding his white three-speed Schwinn bicycle back and forth in front of me taunting me with names I don't remember any more, but they evidently stung sufficiently at the time to awaken those fatal comparisons being generated by my wounded heart. Finally having enough of it, I picked up a rock and threw it at the demon that was trying to make me *less than,* and Gary just happened to be in the way. Naturally, fate guided my one and only throw, and Gary's grin melted into a surprised howl as the rock struck him square on his eye tooth. Goliath fell, but I was no David.

Resentment and whatever power I momentarily felt instantly became fear and trembling as I ran home on wobbly, adrenalized legs, terrified of taking responsibility for what I had done. I was feverishly trying to figure out an escape plan when Gary's mother called. After she hung-up from blasting me in the ear over the phone, my memory banks are blank. I don't remember what she said, only the tone of her voice and my inner frozen fear.

The carefree childhood spirit of our friendship had been threatened by the impulse to settle a score, but now it was irreparably damaged by my greater need to avoid taking responsibility for it.

By God's mercy, I ran into Gary on a plane flight from another city some fifteen or twenty years later. We sat together and reminisced. I remember seeing the brown spot still on his tooth indicating receipt of the message my rock had delivered that day. The consequences, as with so many impulsive actions much regretted afterwards, had left a permanent result. Curiously, he had never had a dentist repair it. A theologian once reminded me of the obvious: Jesus was raised with the scars on his body still visible. I had never considered that connection before. How could I miss that? Sin is forgiven, not forgotten.

Like the beautiful animal on loan to me in my dream, every child's spirit is carefree and joyous when the heart is pure and light, undefiled by comparisons and the jealousy and envy they spawn. Demons of revenge are never satisfied. I hope I apologized to Gary at some point. I really don't remember. I wish I did, but chances are if I didn't, he and others like him, will visit me again someday as in a dream…in this world or the next… until the carefree souls we were both blessed with in the beginning have been fully restored. That kind of visiting scientist is like a messenger from Heaven, inviting me to settle the score a different way. "Unless you enter the Kingdom of

God as a little child, you shall not enter in."[1] Confession
and asking forgiveness are painful and even foolishness
to one who seeks an eye for an eye and a tooth for a tooth,
but they save the world from becoming, as Ghandi observed, one where everyone is toothless and blind. Confession and repentance are the antidotes for the weari-
ness of the fugitive's flight from the one he has wounded;
a flight which is ultimately away from his own being.

---

1 Mt. 18:3.

QUESTIONS FOR DISCUSSION

1. Whom in my life have I injured in some way and not turned and asked forgiveness, and sought to make amends?

2. Do I cultivate gratefulness and thanksgiving for what is given, celebrating the gifts of God however they are bestowed? Do I compare myself with others and become critical of myself or another because of the differences I find?

3. Am I able to give thanks for and bless my enemies, seeing the pain they cause me as a gift of God revealing to me my own sins and afflictive emotions that I need healing from? If not, what does my refusal to show mercy reveal to me about God's place in my life?

Shark-Tooth Grace

The mind cannot control the present moment, the time during which things can arise, so it pretends that it does not exist. This causes a person to behave in a completely unconscious way, forcing the individual to wait for the mind to absorb an event (which by then has become an event in the past) before she or he is allowed to experience it.

Archimandrite Meletios Webber

As a young boy I used to scour the beach for sharks teeth; the black prehistoric kind, polished smooth by the sea over centuries. In North Myrtle Beach in the 1960's you could find a dozen in an hour's walk. Imagine how many creatures must have lived in the ocean for that many teeth to float ashore daily? I have given up trying in recent years, because they have become so scarce.

During a vacation some forty years later, I was walking that same stretch of beach I had as a boy, pondering the way I had been working lately and what effect it was having on my creativity. I noticed a young boy scampering over the sand to his father. "Daddy! A shark's tooth!" His little legs skittered over the surface like pinwheels fanned by the excitement of his discovery, while his eyes

Edited from an article first published in *Columbus Ledger/Enquirer — Health Advantage* supplement, Feb, 1999.

fastened on the gleaming black jewel held carefully in his little sandy fingers.

My thoughts melted away, replaced by joy in my heart for that little boy. His love for his father and his gleeful delight reminded me of a time when I was that father and my son was that boy. I was warm all over for a second and then the Grinch appeared with his minions and began stealing Christmas from me.

A subtle thought arose from the mist, "You have joy for another person's joy." I was just starting to react to this spiritual growth temperature-taking when something recognized the intruder for who he was and sounded the alarm: "Danger! The thieves of spiritual pride and vainglory are penetrating the perimeter of the heart." I let it go. Instantly another phantom was there to take its place. The demons always use a tag team match to trip up wandering pilgrims who stray too close to the truth for their comfort.

Before I realized what was happening, I was scouring the beach looking for a shark's tooth of *my own*. "If that little boy can find one, then I can too." I became aware of the intensity with which I was now searching which contrasted with the lightness and relaxed joy of moments before. I noticed it had some of the same compulsive pressure with which I had been working in the past few months, that was sapping my creative energy to write and to ponder and pray.

Creative writing (and living) is very difficult when we get too far out of balance between relaxed play and intensely focused work. My searching had that anxious,

striving, acquisitive, intellectually driven quality associated with what we pastoral psychotherapists call "working too hard." It's what happens in our profession when
we forget that we are co-pilgrims with other persons who
discover how to solve their own problems. Instead, like
Moses striking the rock,[1] we feel the need to solve things
for them, inevitably putting too much stock in our own
knowledge and past experience instead of trusting in
God's invisible work in another's life doing a new thing.
We are not mechanics or surgeons who take it upon ourselves to "fix" the patient-as-passive-inanimate-object,
but more like midwives who stand in awe of the mystery
of the birthing and rebirthing of the human soul in the
midst of temporary pain.

Within seconds of noticing this and letting it dissolve
like the water seeping into the sand along the shore, I
began wondering why my joy in the little boy's delight
wasn't enough for me. Why did I betray it by succumbing
to the need to possess a shark's tooth for *myself*? Isn't it
just as good for me that another person on this earth has
a joy as for me to have it? Are we not equal in God's eyes?
Is the earth not one home for us all? Do we not ultimately
share everything? One person's joy is another's joy just as
another's loss is my own, just as every sin against another
is a sin against Christ who is the shared life of all persons.

Now I began walking as I'd earlier set out to do, letting go of all this every time I became aware of and just

---

[1] Num. 20:11.

breathing in the sweet, warm, salty air, cracking tiny shells beneath my feet and feeling my toes spreading the wet earth. The sea was bright blue-green, a virtual television set broadcasting the location of the fish underneath the surface to the winged hunters above. A group of old brown pelicans moved silently in tandem with the force of the wind, nose to tail, linked together in formation like the tip of some ancient spear, soaring above the luminescence, scanning for shivers of light that announce the menu for their breakfast. Skimming the surface, they open their mouths sifting the water and then rising up brimming with basketfuls of life.

On my return, some thirty minutes later, the thought occurred to me that my writing is best when I just let it emerge without the intensely pressured focus that I was using earlier when I was anxiously searching for the shark's tooth, my eyes no doubt blinded from the oily vapors of greed burning around the edges of my heart. I realized I'd had too much of that effort lately; too willful and driven. I needed to return to trusting God, and letting life emerge from moment to moment without worrying about "storing up extra corn (or shark's teeth) in the barns of my selfish ego." I wanted to travel light — like the Apostles and the pelicans — free to live and let God take care of provisions.

Quietly and without thought at the moment when my heart felt an uncluttered serene release, I happened to glance down and a tiny little shark's tooth *leapt* into my vision as if planted by an angel for me confirming the link between the inner and the outer with perfect timing. Finding a shark tooth at that moment had been the far-thest thing from my mind. I hadn't even thought about a shark's tooth for the last half hour. I laughed and felt an appreciation for this gift confirming the rightness of my silent intuition *at just that moment.*

"Seek ye first the Kingdom of God and His righteous-ness, and all things necessary shall be added unto you as well."[2] And "Unless you become like little children you shall not enter the Kingdom of God."[3] The little boy, his father and the pelicans were long gone by now. As I con-tinued walking, the boy I once was and the man I hope to be now traveled together holding on to a small piece of wonder. A once white razor-sharp messenger from the gaping maw of a prehistoric behemoth, polished and rocked by the ages, was born to the shore out of an an-cient maternal womb. Alone on the shore, now a shin-ing black pearl, shorn of the sting of death, becomes a small light-bearing witness to the Way that leads to Life through the Father and the Son. Glory to Thee, O Lord.

---

[2] Mt. 6:33.
[3] Mt. 18:3.

QUESTIONS FOR DISCUSSION

1. In my daily work and responsibilities, do I move at my natural rhythm, with prayerful presence as the foundation of what I do or rush around in response to pressures and self-imposed demands that disrupt inner peace?

2. What small unexpected gift of grace this week has confirmed God's presence in my life in a personal way so that it helped restore my natural rhythm?

3. What can I do to "become as guileless as a little child" in my heart, living in the present moment where everything is gift never before experienced and having joy for the joy of others as though it were my own?

Pavanne at Day's Beginning

I stand in awe of the many "coincidences," "chance" meetings, synchronicities and fateful detours that have impelled and guided me on my life's journey.

Peter Levine

Jesus asked, "Were not ten cleansed? Where are the nine? Was no one found to return and give praise to God except for this foreigner?

Luke 17:17–18

SEVEN O'CLOCK. IT'S STILL DARK AS I PULL out of the garage to work. NPR drones on, but I feel like hearing some blues this morning. I have a slight headache and my face feels a little swollen from sleep. Fumbling in the dark for the old cassette tape, I put it in and rewind. Wrong one. The melancholy strains of Ravel's "Pavanne for a Dead Princess" spread gently like a South Sea island sunrise in my heart, melding the deep blue violet of the ocean with the thin red line of light awakening the world. I haven't heard that melody in ages. I didn't even realize it was on an audio-tape, it's been so long since I have heard it. I decide to listen to it anyway, telling myself, "This is what the morning has brought. God is in this."

Edited from an article first published in the *Columbus Ledger/Enquirer — Health Advantage* supplement, June 1997.

In the midst of five-year strategic plans, longer work hours and bottom lines that rise to the top of decision making and hit people over the head knocking them out of the line up like so much chaff, it feels good to know that even what is unplanned and seems like a mistake can be a harbinger of good news. In accepting the "error" as a gift, I am blessed. Meanings emerge from the unconscious like caterpillars pouring forth from a springtime cocoon, bringing spontaneous fluttery intimations I could not have created by my own willfulness no matter how hard I try. Grateful expectation is a powerful force.

The sweet poignant melody continues and I let my mind meander and drift, remembering many years before when this song meant so much to me. Suddenly I become aware of the date and, lo and behold, it is fifteen years *to the day* when our six year old was run over by a car. "Pavanne for a Dead Princess." I smile at the name, wondering if it is being played in her honor this morning and who did so. Tears move like a gentle wave from the middle of my stomach up through the chest and touch my eyes, receding like the tide, disappearing into sand and sea.

Still ringing like a bell with the life elicited by this coincidence, I bring the tape in from the car and play the rest of it in my office as I sit down at my desk. There is too little music in my day.

On the wall in front of me is a picture taken from the cover of an art textbook my wife used when she was finishing her college degree. It shows the exhibit of the Russian painter Mark Rothko and the unmistakable architecture of the spiraling Guggenheim museum in New York City designed by Frank Lloyd Wright. I discovered the book from which it was taken, lying on our coffee table at the time. I remember looking at it and wondering to myself... "The Guggenheim museum... That's the Russian artist Mark Rothko's exhibit, the only exhibit I had ever seen at the Guggenheim in my life"... and thinking it strange that it should be on the cover of a book.

But then, stranger still, my eyes telescoped to the center of the cover to a figure just above the words "second edition." There I am, standing at the rail, looking out over the museum, my sleeves rolled up part-way, with my tall, skinny and brilliant friend Gordie standing beside me. At that instant it dawns on me, "I am Claudia's *second edition* husband." I laugh at the oddness of the salutation — a picture of me taken years earlier now finding its way on to the cover of an art book that happens to be the text used when my wife takes the course at the local college!

Dr. C. G. Jung coined the word *synchronicity* to mark those marvelous events in the universe that are non-causal and yet related to one another significantly in meaning. I wonder at the meaning that is just out of reach to me at this moment, but not out of reach of the joy it elicits and gratefulness to the Author of all things. Synchronicity points to the larger fabric of our lives as being one great piece of cloth whose warp and woof is woven together by threads of One whose life is as important to each particle of the whole as oxygenated blood is to cellular life in the body. Meaning reveals Spirit that we share. Spirit breathes us. It invites us to live not as gods who are in control of the breath of the world, but as recipients of a great privilege and grace. We are beings who belong together, both the living and the dead, those born before and those who will be born after us, in ways that we can't fully fathom and yet we cannot deny. What does this ask of us?

As I finish this meander, Debussy's "Daphnis and Chloe" has faded and now the sweet strains of Ravi Shankar's sitar bless the space. The invisible breath of life this morning has plucked my heart like a string. It is not yet eight o'clock but I am primed to continue a day that is revealing itself to me as a gift from an intimate friend and complete stranger at the same time. I am reminded of a cloud of witnesses from this world and the next for whom faith, hope and love abide, each testifying to a *Presence* beyond our own, that values each of us in a personal way, attentive to the smallest detail, yet so meek as to easily go unnoticed.

Questions for Discussion

1. Something breathes me and causes my heart to beat. I am offered consciousness by One who is already conscious of me. What is my response to this? Can I experience it rather than merely "know about it" with my intellect?

2. Do I believe that God is aware of me every moment? What gift has God given this week which I have failed to be thankful for because I have taken it for granted or attributed it to chance or luck? What makes me ignore God's presence in my life?

3. Do I believe that loved ones who have died are alive in Christ? Do I believe we will all face a 'last judgment' and be alive bodily after death? Why or why not? How does this belief influence the way I am living my life now?

Not a Dog's Life

We need today more than ever before, precisely a 'band of spiritual firebrands' who can inflame minds and hearts with the fire of a loving knowledge of God and Jesus Christ, the Redeemer.

Fr. Georges Florovsky

UNLIKE MY SON'S IGUANA, BRUTUS, WHO seems to remain himself through all circumstances, our miniature long-haired dachshund doesn't quite understand he is a dog. I guess it's hard to realize that when you're around people every day who talk to you and love and play with you so that you will never again be satisfied with a dog's life. Whenever a member of the family walks in the door Eli becomes hyperactive, bonging about on two legs like a spring trying to jump high enough to kiss us on the face.

But then there is the grill... Eli loses his humanity when he hears the click of the gas grill and he *instantly* flames on with an incessant staccato of screeching yelps and shrieks meant to demand, plead, beg, threaten and pray his way outside at once! He is totally focused. One-pointed. The grill is god and Pavlov was his prophet! The sound of the gas flame being ignited transports Eli to the prehistoric edges of his being where wild dog is clearly visible on the horizon. Add the smell of meat cooking and whatever humanity was evolving dissolves as cleanly as a soap bubble in tap water. Turkey is especially serious business. I throw it in the yard. My fingers are too valuable.

I am ashamed to admit that sometimes I find myself listening to his yelping and secretly enjoying his frustration, fascinated by his all-consuming desire. It is funny and pathetic at the same time. He reminds me of me. What do I demand, plead, beg, threaten and pray for all at once with every ounce of being in me? God? Sex? Money? Family? Pizza? Under what conditions do I lose my humanity and revert back to my most basic, pre-cortical neanderthalian instincts for self-satisfaction?

On the other hand, I'm so tame, so often. My prayers and my love don't usually have the ooomph that Eli's do. When I am aware of the unspoken dimly heard cries locked inside me, I sometimes feel like I imagine Eli to be at such moments. Helpless, but not without hope—cut off from what I yearn for more than anything else, precisely because I feel so close! It is at such times that I am more likely to salivate for my turkey, shut behind the glass door of seemingly impossible human limits, yearning for the eternal. Unlike Eli I grow tired of waiting for the Master to open the door and become absorbed in other pursuits. I wish I could demand, plead, beg, threaten and pray like Eli does; insistently, achingly, incessantly, until the Master opens the door if only out of irritation to stop the noise!

Why would the Creator take a high-powered, interactive, self-regulating computer and connect it to a lizard that lives only to eat and reproduce, by way of warm-blooded feelings encased in a sensitive garment of skin with expressive, soulful eyes? What purpose does this serve in the universe? Brutus can't depart from his instinct. Lizards are cold-blooded. Eli is warm-blooded, but feelings alone won't raise him beyond instinct to what William James called the realm of the "twice born" — those who have fed on spiritual food and glimpsed a new way of living in our same old world.

Homo sapiens is an intersection of Spirit and biology in which lizard, dog and rational self-awareness have the potential to become transformed into something utterly unique: *person*. It's a potential, not a guarantee. The danger is that the whole enterprise flops because the creature prefers self-worship in the form of obeying its instincts disguised as if they were gods and goddesses. The results are disastrous. As Mark Twain once said, "No animal is capable of being as beastly as human beings." But when the instincts, feelings and thoughts are transformed by interaction with the Spirit, the universe receives a great gift. Such a person becomes an instrument of peace, wonder and thanksgiving. Impressions of life enter into the person, both good and bad, and are converted into ripe fruits of the Spirit. Love, humility, patience, self-sacrifice and praise blossom forth, bringing blessing to all Creation.

What makes the difference in the success or failure of God's experiment to produce a person? Perhaps I will never know unless I am willing to search and pray like my dog, not for turkey, but to hunger and thirst for my

daily being bread that creates the human *person*. What
kind of effort is demanded? And for how long? I begin to
discover that as hard as I try, I am incapable of making
such a sacrifice consistently through good times and bad,
in plenty and in want, through sickness and health, in
pleasure and in pain. But this is not what God requires,
to go it alone entirely on my own. Jesus did indeed call all
people to "be perfect as your Father in heaven is perfect."[1]
The word translated as "perfect" is *telos*, which means to
reach the end and final purpose for which we were created. St. John Climacus made a comforting observation
in this regard. He said that in this life "it is not possible
for all to become passionless;" that is to reach the pin-
nacle of perfection, "but it is not impossible for all to be
saved, and to be reconciled to God."[2]

Salvation. What is this? It is the flame of love for God
burning brightly in the heart, warming it toward all creatures great and small, that arises to the degree that the
heart has been purified of all idolatry by the Grace of God.
St. Basil describes this as the Divine eros experienced as
a "piercing and unbearable love produced by God in the
soul which has been purified of every evil."[3] Such perfection arises through having been approached first by

---

[1] Mt. 5:48.
[2] Cited by C. Carvarnos, "The Orthodox view of Salvation," in
C.N. Tsirpanlis (Ed.). *Orthodox-Unification Dialogue* (New York:
Rose of Sharon Press, Inc., 1981) p. 60.
[3] Cited by Archimandrite Vasileios in *Monastic Life as True Marriage*. (Alexander Press: Canada, 1996) p. 11.

God and having tasted the bread of heaven. Which do I hunger and thirst for more — the righteousness acquired through relationship with God or to have my turkey and have it NOW!

Love is not the result of willful force, intellectual comprehension, meditation methods or esoteric practices. Regardless of what results are achieved by human effort and design alone, it is the encounter with the One who *is* love that proves transformative. This is the door through which we enter into eternal life and only a guileless reception to what is freely offered by the Giver of Life to all who wish to receive Him, born of the defeat of the so-called self-made man can bear us through it.

QUESTIONS FOR DISCUSSION

1. Is there anything or anyone I demand, plead, beg, threaten and wish for in my life with every ounce of my being?

2. Who in my life relates to me in ways that awaken and encourages me to passionately seek to be in Christ?

3. When I pray, do I know how to be still in my body, mind and heart? Is my prayer more of an attempt to get God to listen or an act of deep attentiveness to the faith that God is already present? How do I become *present*, NOW?

Birds on a Wire

In everything there is an unexplored element because we
are prone by habit to use our eyes only in combination with
the memory of what others before us have thought about
the thing we are looking at.

Guy de Maupassant

I HAVE BEEN NOTICING BIRDS HOLDING COURT
on telephone wires these days — wing to wing by the doz-
ens — all scrunched together at one end near the pole,
while there is plenty of space elsewhere on the wire.

This morning on the way to work I was imagining
having a telescopic lens and taking just the right angle
on them to make a photograph. That thought was followed by one reminding me that there have been many
others who have photographed birds on a wire. There
is even a movie with Goldie Hawn and Mel Gibson
called Bird on a Wire. "What has been will be again,
what has been done will be done again; there is nothing new under the sun ..."[1] whispers in the background
of my thoughts.

Sometimes when I begin noticing things like this, I
become aware of myself noticing and being aware *that*
I am aware. Noticing the noticer has become something

---

[1] Ecclesiastes 1:9.

that increasingly calls to my attention. Yes, there have been birds on a wire before, but no, I have *never* noticed them in this exact way at this exact moment before. Most importantly, I have never noticed myself noticing them at this moment. Hmmmm.

My son told me that when he was a young boy he had to stop himself from thinking about 'What comes after the last number you can think of?' because he used to get so deep into the question the endless looking began to make him anxious. Smart boy. Infinity is one of those imponderables that sends computers (and perhaps six or seven year olds) into negative feedback loops they can't get out of. That's because they weren't designed to contemplate. *We are.* But contemplation is much more than an extended linear process. It means giving up holding on to our observations of the objects we notice and becoming more interested in the noticing. Like the simple words attributed to Jesus in the Gospel of Thomas, we must learn to "become passersby."[2] An old Zen Haiku conveys a similar truth: "The wild geese do not intend to cast their reflection. The lake has no mind to retain the image." Machines aren't conscious and can't be aware of noticing themselves noticing. They are doomed to eternal recurrence until they burnout because they cannot let go of the attempt to retain what has already been witnessed. They continue in an infinite monologue trying to explain everything

---

[2] Gospel of Thomas, Saying 42

in terms of what they already know and have experienced, regardless of how many times they go over the same ground. *You* and *I* have other possibilities.

When couples get in emotional negative-feedback loops arguing in their relationship where each is trying to change the other in order to feel better, they frequently can't stop and inevitably begin to suffer more, going round and round, louder and louder like in a squirrel cage. Psychiatrist R. D. Lang wrote a book of poems called "Knots" celebrating the intricate emotional pretzels he found that painfully tied unhappy couples together. Here's one.

> How can she be happy when the man she loves is
>   unhappy?
> He feels she is blackmailing him by making him feel
>   guilty
> because she is unhappy that he is unhappy.
> She feels he is trying to destroy her love for him by
>   accusing her of being selfish
> when the trouble is that she can't be so selfish
> as to be happy when the man she loves is unhappy.
> She feels there must be something wrong with her
> to love someone who can be so cruel as to destroy
>   her love for him
> and is too guilty to be happy,
> and is unhappy because he is guilty.
> He feels that he is unhappy because he is guilty
> to be happy when others are unhappy

and that he made a mistake to marry someone
who can only think of happiness.[3]

The therapist tries to help the couple dissolve the
pretzel by being willing to enter into the vulnerability and
emotional transparency the pretzel is designed to help
the couple avoid. Why can't they do this on their own?
What is missing?

Freedom from the same-old, same-old stuck repeti-
tions of daily life is what happens when the heart that
wonders at the world begins to take precedence over the
insatiable information-collecting and ego-protecting
mind that fears dwelling in the heart. The resulting emotional reactivity due to mindlessness makes pretzels out
of our daily lives. Wonder is born of being noticed by
someone other than ourselves — not the egoistic "to be
seen of men"[4] variety mentioned by Jesus, but the One
who always re-members us in silence.

When "I" am present writing this and "you" are present reading it, what is occurring "between" us? In English,
the word "love" is what links "I" and "You." Recognizing
that love is the "between" rather than something you or I
do alone, existing merely as a part of our 'subjectivity' we
discover that we can only become ourselves in relationship to an "other" who is not us. Most ancient cultures
call the source of this transformational encounter the
"heart." In Thai, the word for "understanding" literally

[3] R. D. Laing, *Knots* (New York: Vintage Books, 1970) p. 28.
[4] Mt. 23:5.

means "to enter heart." In ancient Egyptian hieroglyphs, the character for 'intelligence' is a heart. Ancient Greek and later Christian hesychasts distinguished between the intellect as *dianoia* or rational discursive thoughts and the intelligence of the *nous* or "eye of the heart" which has the character of a direct contemplative awareness that can be expanded and enhanced by the indwelling energies of God that penetrate it from outside of itself precisely at the place of "meeting" between I and Thou. In other words, our consciousness is not the source of itself. We come into being through dialogue with an "other." It is this encounter which always accompanies what seems like consciousness of "myself." The truth is "I AM only when THOU ART."

When I am noticing birds schmoozing in unconscious intimacy along a wire, it is equally true that I am being noticed in the act of noticing them. I may or may not be aware of this — usually not. Behind the camera's eye is an "I" that frames the picture and values it. Birds on a wire become a wondrous, beautiful sight never before seen, because behind the "I" that is noticing them is a Thou Who frames and values each one of us our whole lives long, whether bunched together on wires or in any other situation, and never, never attempts to capture or hold us against our will.

I AM only because I am re-membered by God. We are being breathed in the act of breathing, being known in the act of knowing, and being loved in the act of loving. Stunned to awe by the never-before experienced glory of such moments, it is natural to try and capture it in a picture. But glory is what gives everything else its evanescence — an invisible, uncreated light revealing all things, a soundless voice echoing through the ages in between the discrete moments of consciousness where subject and object arise, whispering the refrain in all places and filling all things, "This is my Beloved Son, Listen to Him!"[5]

---

[5] Mk. 9:7.

QUESTIONS FOR DISCUSSION

1. What do I know personally about what the Psalmist means by "Be still and know I am God."

2. Try an experiment. Be still for a few moments and do not move a single muscle. Sense your whole body. Notice what is around you without looking around. Listen to any sounds that are present. Breathe naturally. Allow yourself to be free of attachment to whatever thoughts arise, simply noticing how busy the mind is. After a few moments, put the question to yourself, 'How do I turn to the present moment?" How do I notice the noticer? Try this together for ten minutes and then stop and discuss with each other what you discover. See if you can notice the difference between attentive presence and your ordinary way of being.

3. Is love "inside us" or "between" us? Why or why not?

Dia-Logos with the Cosmos

What is man that Thou art mindful of him or the son of man that Thou visiteth him?

Psalm 8:4

Eternity knows no duration of time but contains in itself the full compass of the centuries. Eternity without space includes in itself all the expanses of the created world.

Archimandrite Sophrony

Astronomers recently discovered a planet 600 light years away from earth with 70 degree temperatures in just the right position from its sun to support life as we know it. A mere 600 light years is of microscopic proportions in comparison to the estimated size of the known universe which is already infinite and still expanding. Beyond that, we do not even know if ours is the only universe there is.

A light year is one of those concepts we use as if we know something, yet are totally unable to comprehend what we are saying in any meaningful way that connects with our experience. There are so many such imponderables in our lives that to go about thinking we are in control of anything or that we understand how the universe all fits together is a sure sign of madness.

Edited from an article published in *Columbus Ledger/Enquirer* – Health Advantage supplement, June, 2001.

I was watching a small ant careening back and forth over a stone on the walkway recently. It was moving fast — perhaps 14 or 15 times the distance of its own body in a second. If a six foot man moved 15 times the length of his own body in one second he would be able to keep up with cars on the highway at speeds over 60 mph.

"Now wait just a darn minute!" you say. "If that were the case, you could hardly even see the ant moving." Relativity is all about scale and proportion. The ant only looks slow to us because we are giants on a scale logarithmically beyond the world of the ant. It's not unlike how jets appear as tiny stars blinking in the night sky, barely seeming to move.

Some physicists have recently confirmed that neutrinos, part of the sub-atomic world that comprises the basic substance of the known universe, have been clocked moving close to Einstein's now proverbial speed of light. Think about it, these little Olympian wave-particle dualities are flying around in our bodies at speeds we can't comprehend let alone notice.

Relatively speaking, there is as much distance between the electrons circling the nucleus of an atomic particle as there are between the planets circling the sun. These 'clouds of energy' are what constitute the molecules that comprise the cells of our bodies. With that much space in between the clouds of energy and wave-particles racing through our bodies, we shouldn't even be able to see ourselves. Come to think of it, maybe we could make that trip to that new planet discovered only 600 light years away after all, if only we knew how to switch back and forth from mass to energy like those electrons...

Appearing to stroll about at 3 miles per hour while spinning round and round, upside-down and right side up in a circle at 1000 mph fastened down only by gravity to the 24,000 mile circumference of the earth, which is itself orbiting the sun at close to 67,000 mph, in a universe expanding outward at 180,000 mph in our sector alone, is a trick few of us would attempt if we realized what we were doing.

The intricate complex balance of all these gyrations is miraculous beyond comprehension. Considering that ants are moving at 60+ miles per hour under my feet while neutrinos pulverize and X-ray the vast emptiness of my body alternately as both particles and light waves while everything in the universe races toward infinity, I have concerns how it is I am able to hold it all together from day to day.

Most of us are accustomed to operating as the center of our individual universes. We do not even break a sweat while managing the many spatio-temporal acrobatics of the greater cosmic dance, blissfully unconcerned how strangely isolated (or privileged) we are. Popular religion often masks our awareness of this stunning reality that might otherwise bring us to our knees in awe. If I "believe in Jesus," (often on the same scale as believing in Santa Claus or the Easter Bunny) I may conclude that this entitles me to an insurance policy for the afterlife while I continue to live however I want without regard for obeying a larger plan than my own self-satisfaction and individual preservation.

When truly troubled by my inability to live by conscience I can calm myself by holding forth with something like "substitutionary atonement!" That's Seminarian-speak for "Jesus took the heat so I don't have too. God loves everybody. Nuff said???" Such casuistry serves as an excuse to go on unawares, doing whatever I wish without any consistent daily attempts to discover the degree to which self-love rules my life instead of a God-centered frame of reference. The real situation is more that we are each flung into life without a choice and then just as we seem to be gaining a foothold, we are yanked out at a moment not of our own choosing and dispossessed of all we have tried to possess in between.

In the publically shared kingdom of 'consensus reality' where reason and materialism are touted as king and queen, it is actually impulsivity driven by pleasure and pain of bodily appetites and the emotionality of likes and dislikes rooted in self-love that hold the power. We eat and sleep, marry (sometimes) and procreate, invent and accumulate things, all the while taking for granted that the world is pretty much the way we see it and want it to be, and whatever isn't, is too far away or blessedly unknown to be relevant to our daily lives. But why would the Creator of the universe go to the trouble of placing such tiny insignificant creatures on such an insignificant planet on the outskirts of the galaxy in a cosmos so gigantic that we'd be afraid we were lost if we weren't so dazzled by all the toys we have to play with in the mean-time? If we live for 80, 90, even 100 years, it is still less than a nanosecond in comparison to the larger scheme of the universe, where the entire 14 billion years of the earth constitutes about a second of cosmic time. Are our ordinary daily lives all we really need to be concerned with?

For five thousand years or more, the prophets of Israel, Zoroaster, the sages of the Upanishads, the Buddha, Al Hallaj, Jalal'udin Rumi and of course Jesus, have born witness to a world that cannot be seen or comprehended by the narrow-minded "man-made" complacency we live 99.9 % or our lives believing in and conforming too. They all tell us that human life is not merely for the survival of species. Life is more than eating and drinking, attending sports events, socializing, marrying and working. Even these activities cannot be all that they might be without recognition of the invisible world in our midst.

When the cosmopolitan, sophisticated, wealthy and well-educated religious leader Nicodemus approached Jesus by night with the opening salvo of "Rabbi we know you are a teacher come from God *because* of the miracles you do" (John 3:2), he was presuming to comprehend the mystery of God on earth according to what he already knew, based on lifelong study, reason and the sense impressions that govern the narrow band of academic, religious, and common-sense knowing that constitutes human life as comprehended by human intelligence. Jesus challenged his presumption immediately. "No one can see the Kingdom of God unless they are born from above" (John 3:3), that is, unless they have encountered the Holy Spirit who noetically awakens us to the presence of an uncreated world permeating and giving rise to this one, where God, who is sovereign and source of all life, communicates with the human heart.

The greatest tragedy of our lives is that we reduce the meaning of our Messenger from beyond the known universe and his prophets, to fit within our paltry socially-constructed and democratically agreed-upon understandings of the world as we already are familiar with it, rather than seek to encounter and be transformed by the One who alone can lead us out of our present darkness into a love and meaning beyond our wildest comprehension.

Apart from this set of magnitudes, Jesus all too easily morphs into insipid cultural shibboleths, redirecting us back to the comfortable and well-worn paths of a meager civil religion acceptable in the public square. The sharp edges of Truth and the authenticity of dialogue with the Absolute God incarnated as human being, are removed in order to seem inclusive and avoid offense. Christian faith is reduced to the magic of Disney-belief in a slot-machine deity who passes out tickets to paradise based on legalistic or sentimental adherence to religious slogans repeated by rote without repentance or obedience.

Or God serves merely as a convenient shape-shifting metaphor for fundamentalist religious intolerance or touchy-feely 'luv' and political correctness that reaches no higher than the natural emotional bonds of family and species that includes those we like, or are related to

by blood, or in mutual business transactions, while ex-
cluding others who challenge the accumulated power
and privilege afforded by being in the world me-first. We
are mono*me*ists pretending to be monotheists.

In order to live all this without being disturbed by
conscience, we console ourselves with what Dietrich
Bonheoffer called "cheap Grace." But the Message and
the Messenger are far greater than this sort of theological
flat-earth perspective. When asked by someone "if only
a few would be saved," Jesus responded by pointing to a
difficult truth.

> *Strive to enter through the narrow way, because*
> *many I tell you, will try to enter and will not be able*
> *to. Once the owner of the house gets up and closes*
> *the door, you will stand outside knocking and plead-*
> *ing, 'Sir, open the door for us.' But he will answer, 'I*
> *don't know you or where you come from.' Then you*
> *will say, 'We ate and drank with you, and you taught*
> *in our streets.' But he will reply, 'I don't know you or*
> *where you come from. Away from me, all you evil-*
> *doers!' There will be weeping there, and gnashing of*
> *teeth, when you see Abraham, Isaac and Jacob and*
> *all the prophets in the kingdom of God, but you your-*
> *selves thrown out. People will come from east and*
> *west and north and south, and will take their places*
> *at the feast in the kingdom of God. Indeed there are*
> *those who are last who will be first, and first who will*
> *be last"* (Luke 13:24–30).

This 'narrow way' begins with *metanoia*,[1] the discovery that as we are, we are not in our right minds. We are not in our right minds because our minds belong in our hearts where Grace can affect us beyond mere words and the illusions of comprehension that console us; where it can change our *being* and our lives.

People who have lost their worldly minds from having personally encountered the Messenger and the Message, begin to travel in a different universe, one Jesus called the Kingdom of God. Worldliness is no longer their primary frame of reference. To consider the reality of an uncreated God who is entirely separate from human consciousness, in whose image we are made, yet who is closer to us than our breath, starts to awaken in us an interest in and response-ability to someone greater than ourselves, who loves the whole creation's riot of diversity that expresses the joy and solidarity of the Creator with beings of all colors, shapes and sizes. One who is seized by this kind of wonder and humility begins a new vocation.

There is a Buddhist saying to the effect that it is rarer to be born a human being than for a turtle swimming in the great ocean and surfacing once every five hundred years, to surface with its neck in a single ring floating on the surface of the water. Perhaps so. I suspect this is true. What a responsibility! Unlike Descartes, it is not wise to

---

[1] Translated into English as "repentance" and usually understood as a one-time change of mind, in actuality it means the transformation hoped for over a life time's struggle to respond to the Divine life.

take for granted that "I am" simply because I appear to think or move or breathe or make money, write a book, run a company, complete a university degree, have a baby or do any other number of things that appear to be "mine" in the small localized scheme of things. The fact is we can be more certain of the existence of God than we are of our own. How then to be responsive to the purpose of God for human life on earth and for my life in particular? What am I here for? What is the aim of my life?

These kinds of questions begin to irritate (or depress) a lot of people if they have to consider them for more than a brief moment. As entertainment they suffice for a while and are acceptable. Like the ancient Athenians observed by the Apostle Paul two thousand years ago, everybody likes a new stimulation, but as a real problem to be considered on a daily basis with the seriousness that Einstein considered finding a unified field theory or with the passion that Jesus pondered over Jerusalem, it is another matter. To consider the reality of God beyond and separate from my own consciousness starts to open up those uncomfortable questions of obedience and response-ability again.

When these questions are sustained long enough, they begin to reveal a hidden world that cannot be known apart from repentance, ascetical struggle, prayer, worship and the humility that comes from being dethroned from the center of the universe. Thankfully, what disturbs our paltry "self-esteem" is also what opens the door before the Great Mystery where the journey begins. It is a *path* that can only be walked by those who have discovered they are paralyzed by complacency and surfeit; can only be seen by those who have discovered they are blind to the uncreated world; can only be heard, by those who are deaf to counterfeit worldly ways, can only be begun, by those willing to leave behind attachment to what is past at the first hint of invitation from the One to whom the path leads in the present moment.

Once having crossed this threshold, when the forces of resistance question me as to who it is that is putting me up to all this — creating these questions and disturbing the *status quo*, revealing to me that I am *in* the world but not *of* it, I shall be very careful with my reply. If I say "I AM WHO I AM" at least I will know that it is not "me" that I'm talking about.

QUESTIONS FOR DISCUSSION

1. Identify and share an experience you have had in which you became aware of wonder and awe at awakening to a depth in the world greater than you ordinarily know. What did you learn from this about the aim and purpose of your life? How did your life change?

2. Is there a difference between doing what I want and doing what God wants? What experiences have taught me this?

3. What are the signs that my faith is alive as a *path* for me in contrast to being used as an excuse for self-calming that justifies me not making any real struggle to depart from self-will in my life? What do I know about what it means to love God above all things and all people? How does this relate to my response-ability for directing my inner attentiveness from moment to moment?

So Fine a Dust

The world only if shared exists.

Tassos Leivathitis

Love does not cling to an I, as if the You were merely its "content" or object; it is between I and you.

Martin Buber

INTIMACY AND WONDER ARE CHOICE FRUITS
from the tree of life. These and others are forbidden to
all who are seduced by the illusions of power and control
afforded by preferring knowledge over the humble act of
listening deeply and attending with humility for what can
only be revealed in love. When asked by his students how
it is that nature revealed so many secrets to him and not
to others, Tuskegee Institute's humble professor George
Washington Carver replied, "When you love something
enough, it reveals itself to you."

The Apostle Paul discerned that love "hopes all things,
believes all things and endures all things."[1] He did not include love "knows all things." Two thousand years later
British psychoanalyst Wilfred Bion paid homage to the
wisdom of unknowing when he advised that the therapist

Originally published in *Radical Grace* (New Mexico: Center for
Action and Contemplation, 2012). Vol. 25(2), pp. 18–19.
[1] I Cor. 13:7.

begin each session with a patient knowing nothing about the person, regardless of how many sessions they might have had together previously. Otherwise, you could be sure the therapist was treating the wrong person!

Wonder and humility accompany profoundly intimate encounters, protecting them like the six-winged seraphim who surround the throne of God. Intimacy's habitation is virginal territory never before lived or known by humankind. In the final days of his life, Rabbi Abraham Joshua Heschel whispered to a visitor that he had prayed to the Lord, not for wisdom, knowledge, or power, but for wonder "and the Lord granted my prayer every day of my life." We walk upon this holy ground with feet clothed by God's Grace in the slippers of awe and gratefulness.

The present moment remains forever untrammeled by humanity's insistence on leaving the footprints of our history as a claim to any territory we presume to have 'discovered' along the way. Like tourists feverishly photographing everything in sight, the jewel of intimacy remains hidden always just outside the fortress of self-preservation. It does not like to have its picture taken. You won't find it captured by the camera lens with the caption "Here I am standing with Ghandiji looking at the Taj Mahal." Or "Here I am inside the Louvre with the treasures of antiquity." Or "That's me talking with God." A priest told me, "I am fearful that if the opportunity arose I might rather have my picture taken with God than to actually have an intimate dialogue with Him." Bless him for that confession that both reveals and comforts me that I am not alone in my vainglorious captivity.

Once I took to my high school prom a girl I had just begun to date and didn't know very well. At 18 years old, my hope of an intimate encounter with "the Word made flesh" was not what St. John intended in his Gospel for sure, although the seed of that Word had been secretly at work leavening me since my mother planted it in my heart when I was too young to remember. What happened that night was a kind of parable that has continued to teach me for forty years.

When she met me at the front door of her home she gushed "I can't wait to get to the restaurant!" At the restaurant, the essence of our dialogue was her exuberance, "I can't wait to get to the prom!" At the prom, vague memories remain of awkwardness and feeling self-consciously alone, but most of all, her now cheery refrain, "I can't wait to get to the party!" At the party … she went to sleep.

The burning coal of the Eucharistic gift arises and passes out of reach as quietly and swiftly as the Lover who approaches the bedroom of His beloved in the Song of Solomon. She notices the feint approach, and hesitates only slightly, for less than a second. Alas, the moment has passed and now she runs through the streets with guileless abandon born of insatiable longing arising from having once tasted the kiss of God's Grace, and seeking Him Who can only be approached when He first approaches us. St. Gregory Nazianzen identifies the paradox: "Who searches for God endlessly has found Him."

Everyone illumined by the Divine Light, comes forward in the fear and trembling of a bride. Able to offer only, "I am who I am," we discover in the encounter, as did St. Paul, that "It is no longer 'I'" but Christ who lives in me."[2] The bridegroom and the bride become one as the Three are One. Meister Eckhart praises the mystery: "The eye with which I see God is the same eye with which God sees me."

Intimacy with God is supported by the arduous ascetical work over a lifetime of seeking to be present in the embodied world which is revealed in its depth only by turning to what seems by contrast, to be God's absence. Prayer is the most difficult dialogue of all; the longest waiting, the deepest emptiness, the greatest helplessness. Intimacy is so much more than relishing the pleasures of the five senses on your first trip to Paris or inhaling the ripe living breath of a Brazilian rain forest. As delicious as these adventures are, in and of themselves they are not intimacy with God. They do not last, but are only momentary pearls of stimulation strung on the string of experience-hunger, a craving for self-renewal through devouring ever more exotic and intense impressions taken in without encountering God in between.

Yet it is God who is sought, knowingly or not, in every encounter. The Holy One is present between us revealing *our* depths through His own. The ascetical struggle of the spiritual athlete includes watchfulness, stillness, fasting,

---

[2] Gal. 2:20.

prayer, remembrance of death, and repentance. All these are designed to render us vulnerable when the Beloved shows up. Preparing for such moments is essential, but they cannot be predicted or controlled by any means.

Archimandrite Sophrony of Essex tells of walking together in silence in the forests of Mount Athos with his spiritual father Silouan.[3] At one point, he casually plucked a leaf from a tree and St. Silouan turned to him and said softly, "Your attention is not right." This profoundly moved Fr. Sophrony who realized at that moment that he had lost his watchfulness and along with it, love for the world. He had fallen back into the desert of forgetfulness; that monologue of self-indulgence which robs the life around him and within him of all preciousness. By contrast, intimacy of dialogue with God is evidenced by the quality of attention and love paid by another Athonite elder to a tiny blue flower when he touched it softly with the tip of his cane as he walked, and laughing gently said, "Don't shout so loud!"

What is the secret of this διά-Λογος with God that reveals the world as an icon of Divine glory? I told an elder on Mount Athos once about my life-long spiritual practices and search. He listened attentively and at one point quietly asked, "And is your ego growing too?"

"Yes," I admitted, the medicine of his loving dispassionate discernment already beginning its work in me. Some years later I shared this conversation with Sister

---

[3] Archimandrite Sophrony, *St. Silouan the Athonite* (New York: St. Vladimir's Seminary Press, 1999).

Philothei, a nun in Greece who I discovered had been his spiritual daughter for forty years. I had asked her "What is the action that we human beings are responsible for in making ourselves available to what God seeks to offer us?" Her response could have been a continuation of the elder's gift to me years before. "The more egotism we have, the younger we are. Christian maturity is to become so fine a dust that when the doors of heaven close, we blow underneath the door like the thief on the cross."

My eyes felt the warm heat of contraction as the rock of my finely honed ego, accumulated and polished over a lifetime, began to give way to a simpler, deeper receptivity in the heart that arises when moved by the One whose humility makes room for lamb and lion to lie down together as friends. I thanked her for that good word and persisted with my question. This time she looked at me and said five very familiar words. I have heard and spoken them often enough in my life, but never before had they reached me with so profoundly revealing and *personal* meaning. "God became human for us." My heart drank in the meaning as the words became flesh and I could not keep back the tears.

We sat in silence together for a few moments, each grateful for the encounter engendered by Him Who cannot be taken by force, but only freely received in the mysterious depths of the heart where all effort is beyond reach. Only faith, hope and love remain and the words of the anonymous prayer we Orthodox Christians pray after receiving the Eucharist becomes honey on the tongue, further sweetening the heart. "Christ our God, you are the true yearning and inexpressible joy of all who love you and all creation praises you."

QUESTIONS FOR DISCUSSION

1. What is the source of greatest joy in my life now?

2. Have I begun to intentionally seek to be present in my life more often? Do I still live in my thoughts looking for life to begin 'tomorrow'? How much time do I waste in front of the TV, on the internet in a dull state of consciousness?

3. Who in my life helps me awaken? Who do I seek out in my life in order to have a dialogue from the heart about the search for God and what really matters? Do I have a spiritual confessor and guide and make regular confessions? If not, why not? Do I *worship* or sit as a spectator?

On Being a Good Husbandman

I will never exchange the dry and dark rocks of Patmos for the flower-lined gardens of Athens. People in the city are without a holy covering. They look at the pretty flowers and beautiful country houses, without their hearts giving thanks to God who has filled us with so many beautiful things. On the other hand, when in a deserted place even the ugliest spot and worst-sounding bird makes you sense God's nearness to you. He who is near God is most fortunate, though he might live on a rock.

Elder Amphilochios of Patmos

When our children were young we lived among the fertile rolling hills of York County Pennsylvania, a half hour from Amish country. We raised chickens, grew almond trees, corn, gigantic sunflowers and made our own bread and apple sauce. We pressed grape juice from our grapevines and ate ripe juicy tomatoes, blue berries, fresh spinach, squash and strawberries from our garden that had been richly fertilized with sheep manure from a local farm and rotted wood shavings from the local saw mill. One day our four-year-old daughter Christi wouldn't eat her fish sticks. She said she didn't like them.

"They like you," I said.

Edited from article published in *Diakonia* magazine, Greek Orthodox Metropolis of Atlanta, 2006.

She protested, "They're dead!"

"You can make them alive again by eating them."

Her six-year-old brother chimed in, "They'll turn into Christi! But part of them won't!" He had obviously been paying attention to at least some of God's grand design.

I said, "That part will go back to the earth and the plants will eat it. In the garden nothing is wasted."

That's how it used to be…for a few million or so years. Our ancestors walked the land as holy ground revering and loving the earth as a precious garden of which they knew themselves to be an integral part. They had names for everything—not mere technological labels—but creative heart sounds like *brother fire* and *sister water* which carried with them the sense of personal connectedness to all living things. Our bodies belonged to the earth whose body was itself part of the great body of the larger cosmos all the way to infinity where it touches the face of God. The Creator's presence in the garden was like a cool breeze, mingling with the breath of our ancestors in an intimate embrace. Everything danced to the music of the Spirit in a full circle around the Creator, each part feeding another to maintain the life of all.

Judging from history and current circumstances it appears that at some point our ancestors lost their sense of belovedness to the Creator and each other. They got too big for their britches and started making decisions without respect for the whole, something which we have continued. The Sacred Circle of life depicted in the story of Adam and Eve in the Garden of Eden was broken. In family systems therapy we use the concept of *isomorphism* to explain how what happens in one relationship gets reproduced in others and *family generational transmission* to talk about how the dysfunction of the ancestors passes down to the rest. The author of Deuteronomy characterized it this way: "The mothers and fathers have eaten sour grapes and their children's teeth are set on edge."[1] From this vantage point we can say that our relationship with God is clearly reflected in our relationship with one another and with Great Nature and vice versa. We can diagnose our problems with God by looking at our problems with the world and with each other.

Increasingly, we live at a too rapid pace in a virtual reality world without evidencing genuine appreciation for how things fit together; one part depending on the rest to be healthy. We turn on the tap easily enough to satisfy thirst, but gratitude remains dried up. "Sister" water denotes nothing more than a commodity to be used so we can justify dumping sludge at sea as if the water 12 miles out won't eventually burn holes in the tongues of bathers 12 miles in, as it has the crabs and lobsters below. Without a twinge of remorse we can eliminate 3,500,000 acres of untouched Tasmanian rain forest as if 400 year old eucalyptus trees are nothing but *lumber* and irrelevant to any function other than the utilitarian interests of number-crunching corporate accountants seeking to feed the inflamed appetites of consumers in order to increase stakeholder's equity.

---

[1] Ezekiel 18:2.

Twelve billion dollars were spent in a single year by a large company employing a cadre of psychologists to study behavior and brain wave patterns to enable them to target marketing more specifically so as to elicit greater demand for "stuff" that is desired by afflictive passions taking root in our hearts. By contrast, the desert Abbas and Ammas instruct us to flee attachments to such things in order to prevent fragmentation and erosion of our authentic love for life and one another. And yet, the very economy of the United States has grown to depend on making sure precisely the opposite happens. Without becoming deeply enmeshed in consumption, many companies and their products would fail.

How can we expect culture to unfold differently than the values each of its members live by? How can we expect to be healthy ourselves — medically, psychologically and spiritually — when our relationship to the rest of life on earth is neither harmonious nor sustainable? We take so much more than we give back, and in modern culture so much is wasted. There is a tension within each of us between exploitation and nurturing which we need to be responsible for, but which we must first become aware of and learn to bear long enough to begin to find motivation to respond. Why? Because a good farmer pays careful attention to the difference in order to succeed not just for the short term but for generations.

"The true measure of good agriculture is not the sophistication of its productivity, but the good health of the land. The standard of the exploiter is efficiency; the standard of the nurturer is care. The exploiter's goal is money, profit; the nurturer's goal is health — his land's health, his own, his family's, his community's, his country's. Whereas the exploiter asks of a piece of land only how much and how quickly it can be made to produce, the nurturer asks a question that is much more complex and difficult: What is its carrying capacity? (That is: How much can be taken from it without diminishing it? What can it produce *dependably* for an indefinite time?)"[2]

The true measure of the health of an organization or a civilization is not its speed, technological superiority, the efficiency of its work force or it's GNP. Rather it is the degree to which each of its employees or citizens understands and owns his or her responsibility for good husbandry. It's the degree to which the Sacred Circle of Life is unbroken because of loving awareness and loving sacrifice for the whole and not just a few privileged parts. The body of the earth and all its life, including the people of every nation is our shared body. We live and die together. What hurts one of us hurts us all.

We are each responsible to the whole for everything we consume and everything we put back in, fish sticks included. In the garden, nothing is wasted. We cannot presume to know and serve Christ without attempting

---

[2] W. Berry. *The Unsettling of America: Culture & Agriculture* (San Francisco: Sierra Club Books, 1977) pp. 7–8.

to heal and preserve the commonwealth of the environment around us and within us. We hear a lot about the global war on terror, but the roots of terrorism have always been and continue to be instigated by "powers and principalities" corrupting the unguarded heart, who like false prophets proclaim "peace and prosperity" while ignoring the fact that it is increasingly only for a few while there is less and less for the rest of earth and of many of its peoples. As we do unto the least of these, we do unto the Lord of all … and so unto ourselves.

Our children are educated first and foremost by what they see us actually choosing in our lives, by what we are doing and how we are responding to those around us. This shows most clearly what we are living for and indirectly, what we are willing to die for. Icons in the Orthodox Church and home are beautiful, but they are useless to us if they fail to teach us to honor the living icons of one another, all around us on a daily basis. In a similar vein, the Divine Liturgy is not an activity that invites us out of our bodies and away from life in the world but is rather a doorway that reveals the way to live in the world as God intends.

Although the seamless union between Spirit and "dust" has been at the core of Christian faith from the beginning of Christianity, and in Judaism before it, discussions have continued to arise over the centuries regarding the role of the body in the spiritual life. St. Gregory Palamas, a former Athonite monk and later Archbishop of Thessaloniki, defended Christian spirituality as practiced on Mount Athos by the hesychasts. These monks, seeking union with God through silence and drawing the mind down into the heart through prayer, in order to be illumined and transformed by Grace, claimed experience of encountering God as person. In contradiction to the teaching of the Western philosopher Barlaam, who argued that the soul must be mortified by punishing the body and that God could only be known through reason, those persons like St. Symeon the New Theologian, who experienced the uncreated Light of God personally, declared that God wishes to bring forth in humans true Passion for life, by purifying our hearts. Rather than drawing us out of the body into purely rational categories without passion, the aim of passionlessness is the transfiguration and integration of all human powers infused by Grace. St. Gregory Palamas corrects Barlaam's tendency toward misanthropy when he observes that "holy dispassion," does not mean a lack of passion or a destruction of the flesh, but rather

> "We (Orthodox Christians), O philosopher, were taught that impassibility does not consist in mortifying the passionate part of the soul, but in removing it from evil to good, and directing its energies to divine things, turning it away from evil things toward good things."[3]

Our hearts will forever groan and ache until this wedding between heaven and earth is consummated. Our children

---

[3] St. Gregory Palamas. *Triads*. 2,2, 19. London: CWS, p. 54.

should *feel* our yearning to love the world as God loves us and see us struggling to pick up our crosses and participate in paying the price of love in our daily lives and choices.

It was the story of these things that caused the hearts of the pilgrims on the road to Emmaus to burn as they talked with a stranger who was later revealed to be the Lord in their midst.[4] This stranger includes the face of every discounted person in every neglected corner of our earth. Apart from becoming good husbandmen who see the unity of all things and are willing to work within creation rather than presuming to stand outside it and gain power and control over it for the sake of profit, the best education, health care and quality of life in the world in and of themselves amount to very little indeed. It is written, "Unless the Lord builds the house (of the soul), those who build it build in vain."[5] So it is with the church of the earth, the church in the home and the church in each of our hearts. Our children's education, just as our own individual salvation, is vitally related to how seriously we give ourselves to this truth on a daily basis in the small corners of our lives over a lifetime which best reflects our real values and our care for those we say we love.

---

[4] Lk. 24:32.
[5] Psalm 126:1.

QUESTIONS FOR DISCUSSION

1. In the garden nothing is wasted. What kind of garden is my life and what kind of gardener am I? What am I trying to grow and what kinds of weeds keep springing up?

2. If my life were being observed by a scientist from another planet, based on what I actually do, and what I am mentally preoccupied with daily, what kind of faith and values would my actions and thoughts reveal? What would the scientists say about what I care about most based on my actions? My thoughts?

3. When it comes to interaction with my family, friends and colleagues, what kind of feelings and interests do I engender by my conversations and actions around them?

Finding Soul Food

The world cannot be an end in itself, just as food has no purpose unless it is transformed into life.

Fr. Alexander Schmemann

ONE OF MY TEACHERS USED TO SAY, "HUMAN beings eat impressions and excrete behavior." Our lives are constantly involved in eating, digesting and eliminating on a variety of levels. The finer the quality of the food, the less we can do without it. A person can survive for more than a month without solid food; a few days at best without water, a few minutes without air, and perhaps no longer than a few seconds without receiving any mental or sensory impressions. But we cannot live at all without the "invisible" food of the living vine of the Spirit.

The other day after a long and stressful morning at work, I punched the wrong button on the snack machine and got a packet full of air with a few potato chips instead of the crackers I had wanted. I hadn't eaten more than two or three when I felt a warm, glove-like well-being envelope me. It surprised me.

Edited from an article published in *Columbus Ledger/Enquirer – Health Advantage* supplement, June, 2000.

Just before, I had been thinking, "I have just paid fifty cents for a little saturated fat that will help clog my arteries and shorten my life span. It will do me no good whatsoever. Do I really need this now? It seemed such a waste. Then suddenly the "drug" kicked in. I wondered, "Was it the oil or what?" I pressed my tongue to the top of my mouth where there was a trace of smooth, salty residue. The devil disguised as a potato chip! Is this what compulsive eaters get hooked on to change their mood? What I really needed was food for my soul. How do I find that?

When I was in college, our eating club agreed to not serve lunch one day and give the money we saved to feed the hungry. I gave money easily enough, but I wasn't willing to forego food for even one meal. Instead, I went to the local drug store for a hamburger and a milk shake, as most of us at this fine upstanding private liberal arts college did. Except for Rich Price. He was a sort of odd duck. Bright. Nerdy. *He actually went without eating.* It was part of his Roman Catholic upbringing. Fasting. It seemed strange to me at the time. His breath was bad. People made fun of him. But we noticed what he *did*. That made an impact.

Rich came to mind again some years later when I was in seminary and had begun seriously experimenting with fasting. I had no idea that abstinence from automatically satisfying every craving could facilitate deeper attentiveness in prayer and refine the senses and awareness. Nor had I any comprehension of how it is possible to get an entirely different view of the human condition by becoming aware of the forces that come into play when there is an active intention and resistance to automatic habit and desire.

I will always remember the taste of the juices of the first grape I crunched in my mouth after breaking a water-only fast on the seventh day, sitting on the roof of a farmhouse in New Jersey. The sparkle and tang of that grape splashing its sweetness in my mouth cascaded throughout my whole body like a tiny exploding nova. All of me seemed interested. As pleasant and powerful as that sensation was, the more nutritious food was the deep appreciation for the act of receiving the life of that grape into myself and wondering at the mystery of the transformations involved from seed and soil into heartfelt praise and love. By being aware of my own physicality and *feeling* it, my awareness was somehow more cognizant of the physical processes my mind could only contemplate.

For a brief few moments, in this collected state, the earth and cosmos became personal and relational. Thanksgiving welled up and spilled over from the cup of myself, offered back to God for every living thing in Creation which depends on this love for our existence. There seemed to be a oneness with all things of which I was a part. When water becomes wine it testifies to the truth that humanity *does not live by bread alone, but by every word that proceeds from the mouth of God.* Extraordinary.

Surely, spiritual well-being involves learning to consistently forego being satisfied with the sleep-inducing junk foods of life which in and of themselves are incapable of awakening the heart to the vibrancy of life. As a result of a flabby and passive attention coupled with the inability to forego immediate satisfactions, we do not learn to appreciate and value the deeper longings of the human spirit hidden beneath the ordinary surface of things. Without collectedness that senses, feels and contemplates in an integrated way, we find it difficult or impossible to digest the spiritual bread offered us daily for our *being.* Without this, I seem to lack interest in creation sufficient to be able to taste and see that Lord is good at any given moment. I cannot *pray.*

My teacher was right. When we receive the foods of our life with deeper attention, the soul is nourished and grows, while the ego is excreted. Failing this, as mere consumers, we nourish our personalities, strengthen our self-centered habits, stimulate our appetites and keep reinforcing our egos (and our pathologies), while the seed of personhood or potential for being in "the likeness" of God remains dormant within us. It is only when the ego yields up first place in the scheme of things, that the soul can be nourished from its sacrifice. It is not enough to merely consume in order to build and sustain physical life. Eating with discernment of the Lord's Body is an act of transubstantiation, a kind of Einsteinian equation describing how created substance becomes the depository for a wordless thanksgiving for a life blessed, broken and given away for the life of the world. Through this mystery of receiving bread for our being we become ourselves.

QUESTIONS FOR DISCUSSION

1. How do I understand the saying "Work as if everything depends on you and pray as if everything depends on God?" Are these two in balance in my life?

2. What is my response-ability in collecting myself—body, mind and heart — through attention, in order to receive God's offering of life in the world?

3. In I Cor 11:30, the Apostle Paul writes, "Anyone who eats and drinks without discerning the body eats and drinks judgment on himself. That is why many of you are weak and ill, and some have died." Could this apply to life as a whole and not simply the Eucharist? What is my experience of this?

Hunting for Life

Reality is to be found not in the pure and lasting but in
the whole of man, not in ecstasy beyond the world of the
senses but in the hallowing of the everyday.

Maurice Friedman

I DO NOT KNOW HOW, BUT MY SIX-YEAR-OLD
son caught a squirrel with his bare hands. My son's exhilaration, the teeth-marks on his finger, and the boy-next-
door's testimony proved it beyond a reasonable doubt.
Even the fear of those *long* rabies needles in his stomach
didn't cause him to change his story one bit.

"So you're the mighty squirrel hunter," said the
amused doctor, who seemed quite familiar with such
cases. Fortunately the painful shots weren't necessary, the
doctor explained, since squirrels rarely live long enough
after contracting rabies to transmit the disease, and there
were no cases of rabid squirrels logged in our area at the
time. Two years later, remembering the incident still
strained the buttons on my son's shirt.

Originally published as "Hunting for Life: A Narrative Examina-
tion of the Roots of Violence in the Pleasure of Killing." *The Other
Side*, 27 (4), 1991, 48–53.

Growing up in the agricultural wilds of southern York County in central Pennsylvania, our children shared their world with animals daily. Deer, raccoons, ring-necked pheasants, rabbits, turtles, chipmunks, moles, black snakes of all sizes, and an occasional fox roamed freely without permits among the neighbors.

Some of our most enjoyable moments as a family have been with animals. Catching toads and slipping them down our shirts has helped us reclaim the unassuming solidarity all young children unconsciously feel with the earth, its mud, and its creatures. Children seem to understand naturally that they, like the earth and animals, have *bodies*. Kids take this for granted; sometimes it surprises adults.

Something inside us comes to life when a deer suddenly appears meandering through the fields in measured attentiveness. Finding footprints like cuneiform inscriptions in the clay transforms a walk in the woods into an archeological expedition. On a cool October evening, the sweet smell of earth awakens my appreciation for the mystery that took place a few nights earlier, when these gentle creatures browsed the corncobs scattered in the fields underneath the moonlight.

For a moment my awe becomes palpable: I am — here and now — *earthbound*, burning with blessings of gratitude and thanksgiving. My flesh and blood are quickened, but not consumed, by an attention whose origin is outside time and space. When *Thou Art*, only then *I Am* and the world is *real*.

I am reminded I am a pilgrim here. I stand on holy ground.

In Matthew's Gospel, Jesus speaks of wanting to gather the children of Jerusalem together as a hen gathers her chicks, spreading her wings protectively around her brood (23:37). I never appreciated that imagery until I saw our little bantam, "Brownie," transformed from a chicken into a *mother* after she hatched her first dozen. Somehow she managed to keep all her chicks under her protection. There is something sacred about that instinctive wisdom, something marvelous and warm in that selfless caring.

The foundation of mature compassion is laid down by having our bodies touched lovingly as infants. Love is given to and through our bodies from the beginning; where this is done inappropriately or carelessly the results are disastrous. Humans who lose touch with their own bodies begin to crave the touch of other bodies not in blessing but in domination. It's not surprising that disrespect for our own bodies leads to disrespect for an other's and this goes hand in hand with disrespect for the planet itself.[1]

I once heard a sermon on the Good Samaritan parable in which the minister used as a central illustration an account of a scuba diver rescued from drowning by a

---

[1] "The ecological problem which is becoming so threatening for God's creation is due to a crisis between the human being and the *otherness of the rest of creation*. Man does not respect the otherness of what is not human; he tends to absorb it into himself. This is the cause of the ecological problem." Archbishop Rowan Williams, from the introduction to John D. Zizioulas, *Communion & Otherness*. (New York: T&T Clark, 2006) p. 10.

big dolphin. After being rescued the man had taken off all his clothes and returned to the water with the dolphin. The man held onto the creature, who took him back to the depths where they played together until the dolphin brought him, exhausted, back to shore. They looked at each other eye to eye in the shallow water for some time; finally the creature made a sound and then joined some other dolphins at sea.

I can't explain why that story affects me so deeply. It has something to do with compassion and humility, with the harmony of life and joy and the grace of God that permeates nature like the air we breathe and the water we share. We are gathered under nature's wings after all.

For all its reputation as being "red in tooth and claw," there is also a sense in which nature is uncontaminated by the awkward high octane and often negative egoism of humankind. In cases like this one, the creation speaks to me of an uncalled-for compassion that puts humanity to shame. Somehow that dolphin represents the simple purity of heart which Jesus says allows those who possess it to see God.

My daughter was two years old when she first held a three-and-a-half-foot black snake that visited us each spring. Every year the children would come running to me at the first sight of this creature who later left his or her (I never figured that one out) worn-out skin hanging in the belfry of the church next door. Although I quivered with adrenalin the first time we saw it, I picked up the snake anyway, determined not to encourage any kind of aversion in my children. I used to place it around their necks when they were little and they would play with it without fear. Only their mother, who could not be convinced that snakes are not slimy, refused to follow suit.

I stopped the other day to pick up a young black snake that was carefully trying to cross the road, listening with its body to the vibrations in the pavement, not comprehending the strange tones of rapidly approaching dinosaurs of steel. It shivered into a ball as my car passed over top of it, and I stopped the car to get out and retrieve it, already imagining how pleased the kids would be.

The snake was almost across the road when I watched a driver deliberately run over it. My heart sank. Why are we so cruel?

Turtles suffer the same fate. Not long ago I stopped around rush hour to try and retrieve a turtle I had glimpsed on a highway near our home. When I got to the turtle I found he was dead, or close to it, with a broken shell. If a rock even half that size had been in the road, only the sleepiest, most unaware driver would have hit it. People routinely drive around such obstacles, choosing their safety and wheel alignment over the thrill of aiming for it and hitting it (the way I, admittedly, sometimes do with old beer and soda cans lying in the road). But what can possess a person to aim for a turtle, a humble creature familiar to every child for defeating the hare in one of the great storybook marathons?

Yet there it is: evidence of the cruel strain running through human beings. It is the cruelty which provokes a man to shoot the toes off a treed raccoon one by one until the creature falls to the ground for human-trained coon dogs to tear apart and then say, as one hunter was quoted in the Morgantown, West Virginia, *Dominion Post* on March 8, 1990, "That's the best part. It's not fun just to shoot them." What is the origin of this craving which demands so violent a touch to penetrate our numbness with a momentary tickle of concupiscent satisfaction?

As a thirteen-year-old, I was hunting for birds along the banks of the Neuse River one day when I saw, on a rock in the middle of the river, a two-and-a- half-foot water snake raised up between heaven and earth like a king cobra, attentive only to the music of the great snake charmer. A small fish of two or three inches, bigger than the snake's own head, was already in the snake's unhinged jaws undulating slowly down its throat. The transubstantiation whereby fish becomes snake, a mystery equaling any on earth or in heaven, was about to take place.

Even as a boy I recognized, if only for an instant, the majesty of the moment. But I soon felt another *serpent* inch its own jaws around my fragile awareness of this sacred time, plunging me into a hypnotic darkness in which I would do its bidding without remorse. I raised my Crossman .177 caliber BB rifle pumped to the max. I was hunting for life — not to be fed by it but to take life to feed my craving for the stimulation which comes from assuming the power to touch life from a distance with the sting of death.

What kind of impulse is this? As a pastoral psychotherapist I study the intricate rhythms of the human heart from both a religious and a clinical standpoint. While biologists watch the outer laws of nature, I watch the inner laws, equally spectacular and strange.

A soldier came back from Vietnam having seen the lead from his rifle splatter brains on the jungle floor and his buddies' knives carving on the cadavers, humiliating the dead. After the experience, it was hard for him to live among friends. Riding the road of his hometown, seeing people sitting on their porches, he said with red eyes that did not permit weeping, "I thought about blowing them all away. That's crazy!" The roar of death-making had all but destroyed the child's heart which could appreciate the bumps on a toad's back as a wonder of wonders.

Food for the heart cannot be digested by that in us which craves the high-adrenalin drug of death-making. It is an addiction — a craving that gradually squeezes the heart from a man, replacing it with stone. One day a soldier is a hero for experiencing this intensity; the next day, when the government says so, the same act is criminal.

We must acknowledge the presence of an unseen, indistinct shadow that can fall across the heart in war, stimulating a craving for death-making that threatens to overcome any originally noble intentions of a man or a nation. The means are varied but the same — there is little difference between poison gas, Agent Orange, sticky napalm, and atomic radiation. We no longer live (if we ever did) with life digesting life to survive as any living creature must do. We live with the cruelty of technical *civilized* destruction hidden inside a collective numbness and sanitized denial that a whole nation can buy into, sending the few voices who try to expose the emperor's naked aggression and lies for the addiction it has become into the courtrooms with cries of insanity. Remember Daniel Ellsberg?[2]

The serpent devouring my wonder and respect for life finished swallowing me before the snake I was watching completed its primal Mass on that hot rock in the middle of the river. I found myself sighting him down the barrel of my gun. Gentle, grateful, wondering hearts do not look down gun barrels, except regretfully in self-defense or to nourish their own life. Even then, they do so with gratitude and respect for the life they must take, careful not to take more than is necessary so that all may live.

My gun-barrel eyes narrowed by hypnotic focus did not notice the colorful priestly vestments of the *Logos* mysteriously at work in that unseen corner of the uni-

---

[2] Ellsberg was an ex-Marine and Harvard scholar first made famous for his contributions to decision theory and behavioral economics. In 1959, he became an analyst with the RAND Corporation and later a Defense Department consultant where he advised the White House on aspects of the nuclear defense program. As a matter of conscience in 1971, he released thousands of pages of photocopies from decision-making briefs related to the Viet Nam War to the *New York Times* and *Washington Post* and the Senate Foreign Relations Committee. Initially indicted on twelve felony counts, charges were dismissed due to government misconduct involving leaking papers of his psychiatrist to suggest he was mentally unstable. His actions helped expose and convict several of the Nixon White House aides and proved significant in the impeachment against then President Richard Nixon. Cf. http://en.wikipedia.org/wiki/Daniel_Ellsberg

verse, that rock in the middle of the Neuse River. Gun-barrel eyes — cold, inhuman, and unnatural like polished steel, refined by science and culture in the deadly arts — intruded upon and transformed the scene. Gun-barrel eyes are silent and attentive with the one-pointed energy of approaching death.

Instantly, one copper pellet opened the back of the little priest's head with the searing pain of metal driven into flesh. Now the undulations are from side to side, around, and over the back, writhing with the strain of conflicting interests. A mouth, stretching wide to receive the grace of life in such largesse that the head, like human ego, had to be intentionally dislocated in order to receive it, is suddenly thrust into the pangs of instinctive self-preservation.

An intentional fast begins immediately. Jaws struggle to release the fish. Life becomes prayer of the only kind possible in such a moment: "My God, my God!" There is no chance for fight or flight or even seeing the shape of one's enemy any more clearly than I saw my own enemy when overcome by the urge to touch that snake with the black magic of a bullet.

I did not begin to understand what I had done or what it was that had come over me, enticing me to eat from the tree of presumption to assume God's place. Not that day.

I repeated the crime of taking life simply for the plea-sure of stimulation until one day when some boys I was hunting with began laughing and driving those same fire-colored nails through the back of a box turtle's shell.

I suddenly began to feel the bite of that creature's wound in some helpless, injured, innocent place in myself. It is the place from which I love my son, "the mighty squirrel hunter," for whom in my better moments I would give my life. It was, as the psalmist says, the child beginning to lead the man.

This child led me to a woods with my friend Andy who used to hunt with me. This time it was a mourning dove, sitting quietly in a tree.

I had heard tales of one of my grandfather's wealthy friends whose sons were several years older than I was and hunted with *real* guns — shotguns. They had talked about how hard it was to hit a dove in flight and how proud that tall, strong, football-playing boy had felt when he finally hit a winged dove with a tiny speck of hot spit from his gun. For some reason I had mentally catalogued shooting a dove as one of the things *real* men do. I wanted to be a man like I thought he was — one who derived self-esteem and satisfaction from using vigilance, patience, visual acuity, and manual dexterity not to give life but to kill.

I got my dove with a single shot. It wasn't in flight, but perhaps that humiliation was providential. Somehow, by God's grace, this dove — maybe a great-great-grandchild of Noah's, with olive juice still in its beak — had been chosen to end my career as a hunter.

The BB fractured the hollow bone that supported her wing. A tiny, bloody tear, a sign of her body already beginning the impossible job of trying to heal the wound, formed around the fatal black pearl. But she didn't fall from the tree. She only shrugged her shoulder as if in forgiveness, and in stillness bore the pain without a single sound.

Her silence echoed the silence of the One through whom she was created, a silence kept long ago on a hill called Calvary. It was like the silence of his grieving mother remembering the embrace of Divine Word and dust that had conceived life and now was uniting the mighty powers of heaven and the fragile vulnerabilities of earth in a single impassioned sacrifice.

We had to shake the bird down. Both of us began to feel wounded ourselves, full of remorse and the fading vestiges of exhilaration that had once brought pleasure to the kill. We pumped the guns and shot again and again, hoping the dove's tearless, open eye would mercifully close and end the agony.

Each shot seemed to pierce our hearts more deeply than it pierced the flesh of the dove. We did not leave the woods until we had conducted a funeral for this fallen herald of God's morning joy.

Funerals are for the living, not the dead.

I realized then, and years later I still believe, that what I truly wanted all along was to be in communion with the creatures around me. I was not even in communion with myself. Grasping at life from the outside, I found only death.

I have since learned of humble persons like St. Francis of Assisi, Elder Paisios, St. Nektarios of Aegina, St. Seraphim of Sarov and the Shivapuri Baba, around whom wolves, bears, tigers and snakes became as lambs. These persons sought to possess nothing, turning to God for everything. Relinquishing all power and control over the lives around them, they found life freely responded to the peace that each of these persons had discovered within through the Grace of God. Even as the winds and sea were tamed by the words of Christ who *is* peace itself (Mark 4:35–39).

We are people familiar with destruction, familiar with the disease of seeking to own the world as mere commodity. Years of useless slaughter of dolphins and whales, pogroms and smear campaigns against foreign peoples, marriage break-ups and emotional starvation of children, obliteration of the rain forests and the remaining giant redwoods, the fouling of the planet itself—these are not new to us. The situation is original only in that it is a continuation of a very old lie. That ancient lie bears fruit in all who have swallowed it and sought to grasp from the outside what can only be given from within.

We live in a time when advanced technology offers the same old seductions — power and speed — in scintillating new disguises. Our invincible technology provides the same old momentary exaltations of apparent mastery over life through the death of anyone or anything but our own pride. It is easy for us to grow insensitive to the humble joy every child seems to experience in communion with creation. As Jesus affirms in a passage from the Gospel of Thomas, "Split a piece of wood, and I am there. Lift up the stone, and you will find Me there."[3]

---

[3] Saying 31 (p. Oxy. 1.30–35).

This God *who so loved the cosmos* is not somewhere far away. This God is among us in the flesh, vulnerable as a child, pristine as a tropical rain forest, compassionate as a wild dolphin, generous and forgiving as the earth, as steadfast and unwilling to desert us as a mother her children, as extraordinary as the miracle of our lives which, like all the rest, we take for granted. To seek life anywhere other than where *I AM* because THOU ART at any given moment is to be deluded, and that is the beginning of death.

To ignore God's sacramental presence personalizing all creation as THOU is to continue our fall from grace. It is another denial of the mercy of Christ which is here and now in our midst, seeking not to change the cosmos but to embrace it so that it can become itself.

As creation was from the beginning, so it continues, and ever shall be — just as God made it — *very good.*[4] Amen.

---

[4] See Genesis 1 for this refrain after each act of creation.

QUESTIONS FOR DISCUSSION

1. What is the evidence in my life that I respect other forms of life that are not human, such as plants, animals and the biosphere of the earth, as expressing spiritual essences and not simply as being commodities to serve human purposes?

2. Have I ever killed another being just for 'sport' or 'pleasure' of it and not in order to live or to defend innocent life? When I kill in order to live, do I give thanks other than in mere words for the life and sacrifice of the creature as well as to God? Do I incur any responsibility to God for the lives I am taking in order to live my own life? If so, what kind?

3. When I receive the Body and Blood of Christ into my own Body, do I pray that my life becomes a passion-bearing sacrificial offering for the life of the world? How am I living this out in my daily life in body, mind and heart? Am I *being* bread for others?

Divine Liturgy of the Forest

We enter the land of silence by the silence of surrender, and
there is no map of the silence that is surrender.

Martin Laird

My wife Claudia and I began our trip
to Oregon by renting a car at the airport and driving from
Eugene to the Oregon Caves. In the morning, we hiked
up a mile or so into the Siskiyou National Forest before
anyone had emerged from the rustic Lodge set fifteen
miles into the forest. No telephones. No TV's. Only one
windy mountain road in.

Stillness prevailed except for the occasional buzzing
gnat. The forest silence is thick and my giddiness at being three thousand miles away from home in the Oregon
wilds quickly gives way to awe and respect. Huge Douglas firs stand like ancient sentinels throughout the forest.
Great arrows shot from the Divine Archer's bow, thump-
ing into the earth with such force, their points split into
long curling fingers reaching down through the black soil,
anchoring them into bedrock. Flaming green feathers

Edited from an article published in *Columbus Ledger/Enquirer—
Health Advantage* supplement, August, 2000.

tower above us as leaves separating the first rays of dawn
into fans of light, arcing down through the forest canopy.
Green moss hangs in wispy patches on the branches and
bark of the older trees like hair on a troll's back. These
trees are bigger than I have ever seen, but nothing in comparison to "Big Tree" as it comes into view.

Climbing briskly up along the path about four or five
thousand feet up, we could feel the effect of thinner air
and it was comforting to realize it was that and not being forty-six years old at the time that was causing me to
be winded a little earlier than I'd expected. Suddenly, before us was the massive giant we'd come to see, an ancient
Douglas Fir, born in 1000 AD, some fifteen feet in diameter. Big Tree towered above the forest canopy, arms spread
wide open, silently turned toward the light, surrounded
by a bevy of new disciples without comprehension what it
takes to live and pray for so long without ceasing.

We sat in silence and listened as a beautiful compli-
cated melody sounded which was answered similarly in
antiphonal style like an echo in various directions, ex-
tending our ear's measure of the forest's depth. It was a
small bird not even as big as a sparrow, who was serving
as priest, belting out a chant in a voice five times bigger
than itself. We were part of a Divine Forest Liturgy. Big
Tree served as bishop — a wise ancient Geronda around
whom the rest of us became the church.

In my heart I felt awe and tender love ready to spill
into tears as I recognized that I loved the woman beside
me from the same place I loved God and appreciated the

blessing of that sacred space and moment. I tried to tell her and botched it, recognizing my puny words couldn't possibly convey the magnitude and nuance of the beautiful moment we were already sharing. Some things are too much for a man to utter. Like Peter on the Mount of Transfiguration in the face of the mystery of our Lord's blazing transfiguration, the tongue moves not in obedience to truth, but in an attempt to capture what can only be experienced without words. In the face of the Divine, it is better to simply be still, trust the Grace of the moment and remember that Christ, the Son of the Living God, is recognizably in our midst. The Word is made flesh yet again. *Listen to Him* while the Spirit bears witness with silence and sighs too deep for words.

We returned from the forest to have breakfast in a 50's-style soda fountain at the Lodge. Hash browns and old-fashioned malted milkshakes tasted great, sidled up to the counter on little red stools, while we listened to sentimental old classics about blissful infatuations. The contrast with moments before, though deafening, was appreciated even more than it would have been if we hadn't drunk our fill of the silence.

Then we moved into the constant forty-two degree ambience of the Oregon Caves. Living rock, growing at less than a dead snail's pace, expands about the thickness of a fingernail every hundred years. Stalactites glisten like ice-cycles dripping in slow motion from ceiling to floor, creating their mirror images rising from the ground. When heaven and earth finally kiss in this way, a column is formed. As the kiss lingers it begins to grow thicker. After a few million years or so it is less than a foot in diameter. All sorts of changes can affect this embrace — earthquakes, decaying trees on the forest floor thirty feet above changing the acidity of the water, air flow through the caverns. The touch of a finger on the surface leaving the residue of oil from human skin is enough to create a blackened bruise on the limestone that centuries cannot remove. Awe again. I had no idea that rock was a life form moving slower than a human being can detect. Only a being living a trillion years or so could see it breathe.

And then the thought, we who live perhaps eighty or a hundred years are born and grow, raise families, sing songs, cry tears and vanish like the Psalmist's grass, too quickly to even be noticed by this ancient mineralized being. Yet in that fraction of a geological nanosecond called a human lifespan, we know that the Creator of all things has breathed the same life into every particle of the whole. We lift up that knowing to the heavens bristling with stars on a black Oregon night and the water of life drips into our spiritual mouths. We are priests who give voice to the groaning of Creation, "Heaven and the earth declare the Glory of God!"

And it was morning and evening, the first day.

After five days full of moments like this one, I understood better why on the seventh day, even God found it necessary to rest and give ponderance to what had been spoken into life. What we cannot keep silence before, we cannot hear. What we cannot hear we cannot embrace.

What we cannot embrace we cannot love. What we cannot love, we cannot live.

QUESTIONS FOR DISCUSSION

1. Recall a moment when have you beheld something so out of the ordinary that you were speechless? What is the difference between that silent presence and the attempt to put the experience into words?

2. What does it mean that "There is no map of the silence that is surrender?"

3. Without silence between the notes, there could be no music. Where is the silence in my life now? How much time do I spend in silence daily seeking to be present? Is it enough to nurture my relationship with God? How do you determine this?

Life at the Edge of the World

The human person "is a being whose essential qualities cannot be grasped by the human mind working within the limits of rational, psychological or sensory perception."

Philip Sherrard

THE OCEAN HAS ALWAYS BEEN A GREAT COMfort to me. Following my junior year in high school, I began spending summers on the South Carolina coast living in the cottage of an 88-year-old retired merchant marines captain. By day I exhilarated in the hot sun, framing houses and feeling the youthful power and delight of good work among other men. Evenings brought a cool ocean dip followed by a feast of stars. The most restful sleep of my life was on a cot tucked away in the corner of Capt. W. H. Whilden's screened-in porch, soothed by sweet, warm ocean breezes and the gentle rhythmical rushing of the waves rearranging the sand like great combs vanishing into dark silken strands ... It was a wonderful coming-of-age rhythm for a nineteen-year-old.

"Cap" was a tall, big-boned man with a deep resonant voice and long white beard, who raised the American flag

Edited from an article published in (2004) in *The Pastoral Forum*, vol. 21, pp. 7–11.

every morning, picked up trash off the beach and played
caroms and checkers with children of vacationing families.
Retired for more than a quarter century, he had navigated
the oceans around the world more times than I had brushed
my teeth. I can still hear his gentle, merry laughter tumbling
out of a good and humble heart that loved life. He had that
freedom from ego that often comes with old age, when the
sap of youthful enthusiasms and derelictions has fermented
into the wine of mature wisdom, gratitude and thanksgiving. Along with the visiting children, he took care of a whole
bunch of cats that kept turning up from every direction.
You couldn't miss the delight emerging from his pixie-like
expression when he lifted them up in huge, gnarled, sea-
weathered hands snuggling them to his face; his big false
teeth flashing white. (At other times I'd see those teeth in a
glass by the sink and he'd be wandering around wondering
where they were. "Have you seen my teeth?!" he'd laugh,
with his mouth all wrinkled and eyes twinkling.)

Sitting silently on his wooden deck, overlooking the
sea, we enjoyed the silent rhythmic rushing of the waves
and the starlit canopy above. Sea oats lining the dunes
bent over prayerfully before the insistent ocean breeze,
providing perches for the occasional "city" birds wandering off course, curious about the vast ocean as if they too
lived there, or might, like the gulls and pelicans.

There are people like those birds in this world — ex-
plorers, poets, gypsies, holy fools — who for reasons
known only to God and perhaps half wise to themselves,
wander off beyond the edges of their ordinary lives, cross-

ing the lines where official maps say the world ends and dangerous Leviathans and sea monsters begin. Lo and behold, they discover, there is more to life than the maps contain! It seems at first almost like a heretical thought. And yet, truth which can be written or spoken is not the Truth, for Truth is the Living One through whom all things were made, the "Treasury of blessings and Giver of life Who is in all places and fills all things."[1] No map can fully describe this Living One. Truth is not a system that can be formulated by human intellect or a doctrine that can be used to neatly tie things up and provide security for small souls who prefer studying maps to the adventure of exploring the territory which they signify. No, the Truth is *alive.* It is not how or why but *who* and *when?*

Metropolitan Anthony Bloom got it right when he observed, "To pray is to enter the den of a lion."[2] Like the ones who ventured outside the cave in Plato's allegory,[3] and

---

[1] From morning prayers, *Prayer Book for Orthodox Christians.* Translated from the Greek by Holy Transfiguration Monastery, Boston, Massachusetts, 2000.

[2] A. Bloom. *Beginning to Pray* (New York: Paulist Press, 1970).

[3] From Plato's *Republic.* By the mouth of Socrates, Plato offers an analogy of our human situation as like persons living chained to a wall in a cave, unable to see that the shadows cast on the walls taken as real, are actually only dim reflections of the forms of persons moving about behind the light outside. When someone escapes this situation and exits the cave, they are blinded momentarily by the light, but soon begin to see what the real situation of the cave is. Returning, they are considered fools or dangerous by those within the cave who cannot be convinced of the truth, because they haven't had the same experience.

were at first blinded by the light of day — William James'
"twice born" souls — these pilgrims, living at the edge of
the world, venturing into the cave of the lion, are forever
changed by their encounters. Regarded as contemplatives
or perhaps exotic and sought out briefly for entertainment
by those who have been faithful and content within ordinary realms, some of these souls find a way to live in both
worlds and some cannot. Another old man I benefited
from a few years later, Fr. Georges Florovsky, in his eighties
at the time, a Russian exile, Orthodox priest and Professor
of Patristics at Princeton Seminary, lived quietly with integrity in this world while leaving noteworthy instruction
for those who would gain a glimpse into the other:

> The Church gives us not a system, but a key; not
> a plan of God's City, but the means of entering it.
> Perhaps someone will lose his way because he has
> no plan. But all that he will see, he will see without
> a mediator, he will see it directly, it will be real for
> him; while he who has studied only the plan risks
> remaining outside and not really finding anything.[4]

And so it is, if the moment is blessed and the heart
receptive, the wind may suddenly catch hold of invisible
strings of the Divine Lyre to announce an approaching
glory; dusk light becomes white hot, burning through the

---

[4] G. Florovsky. *Bible, Church, Tradition: An Eastern Orthodox
View.* Vol. 1 in the *Collected Works* (Europa: Buchervertrieb-
sanstalt, 1987), pp. 50–51.

veil covering the Uncreated Holy Fire of God's love and behold the Bridegroom cometh! Perhaps it was such a moment when William Blake turned to a friend, who had never ventured out beyond the confines of his social and culturally circumscribed world and asked, while looking at the sun, "What do you see?" The friend answered easily, "A yellow orb, of a certain size and presumably a certain distance from the earth, warming us."

From his perch at the edge of the world, riding the back of an invisible dragon rising up from the abyss where I and Thou encounter one another, Blake responded with incandescent wonder, "I see the angelic hosts of Heaven in chariots of fire singing, Holy, Holy, Holy art Thou O Lord God Sabbaoth!"[5]

In the quiet of the approaching night one evening, bathed in the moist mixture of land and sea breezes while cats circled beneath our legs, poems not yet written knocked upon the door waiting to be heard; a life nearly lived in full and one freshly begun, rubbed shoulders and compared notes. It was one of many sought-after meetings at the edge where the film between this world and the next grows thinner.

"Cap, do you ever think of dying?"

Though I had pondered death a good bit, I was still too young to appreciate the twinge in the heart that comes

---

[5] In his commentary on one of his lost paintings, a seven foot masterpiece entitled "A Vision of the Last Judgment," Blake describes one of the visions he experienced that allowed him to see the Hosts of Heaven praising God.

later, when life has been full and there is so much to let go of (or when it has been so painful and hellish that one wonders if death could be any worse). I'd memorized a romantic little poem by Sara Teasdale that I would sometimes think of as I stood on the dunes looking out over the sea from one of my favorite places on earth in front of Cap's Cabin. Each time I uttered the words, something having to do with love and loss and hope and joy and thanksgiving and suffering and freedom and the glory of creation caught in my throat...

> If there is any life when death is over
> These tawny beaches will know much of me.
> I shall come back as constant
> And as changeful
> As the unchanging many-colored sea.
> If life was small, if it has made me scornful
> Forgive me. I shall straighten like a flame
> In the great calm of death,
> And if you want me
> Stand on the seaward dunes and call my name.[6]

I shared the poem with Cap and he was most appreciative, offering me the essential nourishment for further growth identified by analyst Robert Moore who observed, "If a boy doesn't have an older man who loves and admires him, he's being hurt." Cap had written volumes

---

[6] From S. Teasdale, *Flame and Shadow.* (New York: Macmillan Company, 1920) p. 106.

of similar kinds of poems himself while at sea, which he kept in notebooks and occasionally shared with much joy. They were noble and full of affectionate sentiment for creation great and small, and of praise for the wife he had to leave behind for long months of solitude at sea.

He honored me again by considering my question about his own death in silence for a few moments, which were even more precious than his words. Such pondering and self-confrontation made for an intimacy and interest that was the essence of why at nineteen years of age, I thought about death, gazed at the stars and talked with old men on their back porches. It took me deeper toward that untraveled country which sparks in those who have seen its gates from afar, a greater appreciation for the journey in the lands surrounding it.

I have learned over the thirty years since I sat on that back porch with Cap, that death is the mother of every pain we will ever face, the slayer of every joy and the ultimate test of the integrity of our hearts. While we are living, remembrance of death is the foundation of sobriety and prayerful attention. Where faith, love and gratitude are added to the mix, it stokes the fire that heats up the crucible containing our lives enabling a transformation that would not otherwise be possible. Sensuality, pleasure and contentment alone cannot transform a human being. They are insufficient to call forth the kind of heartbreaking passionate love for the world that is God's heart calling to ours to join Him in the deed of sacrificing our pleasure to the point of laying down our lives so that "the least of these" might be included in the very best of God's banquet feast.

It seems that God is willing to undergo eternal suffering[7] for the life of the world. Such love provides fire for the blazing forge in which we become *persons* as contrasted with mere men-machines, winding down throughout our lives like ticking clocks just going through the motions. Without the "lamb slain from the foundation of the world,"[8] without voluntarily embracing the wounding that comes with loving as God loves us, we will never know eternal life.

God did not become human so that humans could avoid the risk of experiencing relationship with God; He did not suffer for love so that we could be freed from the responsibility and privilege real love entails. In Christ the world is offered a place in God's heart, if we want it. We are invited to place ourselves on the altar with Him, sharing the cross because we know that is what gives life to the world and what restores our own life dead from sin. Avoiding the cross only makes the cross heavier for all those who choose to bear it with Him out of love for the sake of the rest.

In the face of life that does not fit our maps or permit our puny strategies to control it, when we discover that apart from God, on the basis of our corporate and egoistic strivings and accomplishments, we are *nothing*, do

---

[7] If there are any persons who are eternally damned, then the suffering of the Lord is eternal as is God's love.

[8] Rev. 13:8.

we succumb to despair? Do we curse God as Job in his immense suffering considered, and endure a bitter, angry, shriveled-up life, living and dying as a mere thing without soul? Do we seek even more desperately to find happiness and pleasure as if we could have it for ourselves while others have nothing? Or do we say "Yes!" to the love and purposes of God whom we cannot see directly but whose Unseen face has brought forth every particle of creation and launched every ship that has ever reached the shores of our souls with its treasures and its woes?" Do we have the heart to stand, as did Job at the edge of our respective maps, facing the whirlwind with the question and call that life has set burning in us until we find the answer which cannot be known without being lived to the end?

The Greek poet Cavafy wrote of life, "Pray the road is long and full of adventure, full of knowledge," but most of all, "Keep Ithaca fixed in your mind. To arrive there is your ultimate goal," yet not to hurry the voyage and not to expect Ithaca will offer riches. After all, Ithaca is the reason for the journey. Without Ithaca,

> …you would never have taken the road.
> But she has nothing more to give you.
> And if you find her poor. Ithaca has not
> Defrauded you.
> With the great wisdom you have gained,
> With so much experience,
> You must surely have understood by then
> What Ithaca means.

We are miracles of life. Yet along the way between
this country and the longed-for, sought-after, Ithaca, everything and everyone we love and invest in, including
our own lives, will seem to slip through our fingers like
the tidewaters vanishing into the sand and we can do
absolutely nothing to prevent this. We can, however, like
a captain on the bow of his ship, look for the invisible
hand of God in each moment as we chart our course according to the north star beyond the edge of the map
of the known world, listening intently for that "still,
small voice of the Lord"[9] at the heart of it all, reminding
"Blessed is the one who is found keeping watch when
the Bridegroom comes, for He shall come as a thief in
the night without warning."[10] It is an odd and arresting
saying from one who moved between the two worlds
with a passion and clarity unlike any other before or after Him. *Keep watch.* Pay attention deeply for a visitation
that comes without warning; that cannot be predicted
and yet is closer to us than our own breath; "Behold, I
stand at the door and knock; if anyone hears My voice
and opens the door, I will come in and sup with him and
him with me."[11]

Keeping watch is a special kind of child-like, guileless, humble, heart-vulnerable, embodied alertness to the
unity of both the known and unknown, the controlled
and mapped as well as the uncontrollable and unmapped

[9] I Kings 19:12.
[10] Mt. 24:43.
[11] Rev. 3:20.

portions of life. It changes the journey. Like the city birds venturing to the shore, it opens the door to visitations of depth of presence that are transformative. Who has seen the purple of a flower so that its vibrance shimmers across the heart in a palpable implosion that is distinct and unnamable, yet unforgettable and calls the heart on the spot to sing a hymn of thanksgiving to God with the fervor that danced David naked before the Ark of the Lord?[12] Who, like Rumi, has looked into the eyes of a homeless stranger and felt the quickening of attention that comes when we realize that in that moment we are being addressed by the Thou of the Beloved and the heart turns inside out with joyful surprise and thanksgiving ready to offer up our last dime in love?

> The Sufi opens his hands to the universe
> And gives away each instant free.
> Unlike someone who begs on the street for money
>   to survive,
> A dervish begs to give you his life.[13]

Who has known the resurrection of Christ, simply by having heard the announcement of one who witnessed the empty tomb and himself believed two thousand years before; who says "Blessed are you who believe and have

---

[12] 2 Samuel 6:16, 20.

[13] Barks & Moyne, trans. *Open Secret: Versions of Rumi* (Putney, Vermont: Threshold Books, 1984), quatrain 686.

not seen."[14] Blessed are you who keep watch for life, for the unseen, who listen to music by attending to the spaces in between the notes out of which creation is eternally generated. As the Chinese sage Lao Tzu observed three thousand years before, while looking in the same direction,

> We shape clay into a pot,
> But it is the emptiness inside that holds whatever we
>   want.
> We hammer wood for a house,
> But it is the inner space
> That makes it livable.
> We work with being,
> But non-being is what we use.[15]

and

> When you realize where you come from,
> You naturally become tolerant,
> Disinterested, amused,
> Kindhearted as a grandmother,
> Dignified as a king.
> Immersed in the wonder of the Tao,
> You can deal with whatever life brings you,

---

[14] Jn. 20:29.

[15] S. Mitchell, trans. *Tao Te Ching* (New York: Harper & Row, 1988), p. 11. See also Hieromonk Damascene, *Christ The Eternal Tao* (Platina, CA: St. Herman Press, 2004).

And when death comes, you are ready.[16]

Though these reflections have taken on greater intensity with the years, they were there in embryo on that back porch. Thirty years later I am even more appreciative of Cap's kindness and affectionate regard for all those he came in contact with on his journey. The loving humble actions of his old age offered testimony of a lifetime of keeping watch from the bow of the ship of his life and repeatedly choosing blessing over curse. His answer to my question whether he ever thought of dying, was simple: He would go down with the ship without regrets, ready for the next adventure beyond the map's edge.

No doubt upon his arrival at distant shore, his heart would open like a ripe pomegranate spilling the bounty of its life treasures at the Lord's feet and by God's grace it would increase one hundredfold as did a little boy's loaves and fishes to bring glory to God and to refresh a hungry world. Such people not only preserve the sanity of the world while they are in it, but when they have passed beyond it to the other side, they become part of the eternal chorus of praise meant only for the ears of God. For those with ears to hear what the Spirit says in return, let them hear!

---

[16] Ibid., p. 16.

QUESTIONS FOR DISCUSSION

1. Have you ever met someone "who for reasons known
    only to God wandered off the map of ordinary life"
    and became alive in a way that inspired you to go
    in search of God, not as an idea, but as One who is
    searching for you?

2. Is death something I cover up and avoid in my life
    wherever possible? Or something that helps me be
    mindful of the preciousness of each moment and in-
    tensifies my prayer and appreciation for life?

3. It is said that "people die, but relationships don't."
    What kind of relationship do I have with Christ? Is
    it as real as the relationship I have with those I have
    loved and who have loved me and have died? Or is
    God more of an idea in my life than the source of
    personhood itself?

Bread and Jesus Prayer
in Northern California

The world cannot be discovered by a journey of miles, no matter how long, but only by a spiritual journey, a journey of one inch, very arduous and humbling and joyful, by which we arrive at the ground at our own feet, and learn to be at home.

Wendell Berry

MOUNT SHASTA LOOMS LIKE A GIANT ABOVE the flat Northern California landscape, rising 14,000 feet in the distance, its snowy white hair hard to distinguish from the clouds surrounding its peak. So much open space. Our hearts silent, enjoying a grateful immersion in wonder and appreciation for this rambling open landscape we are seeing for the first time. Silence thickens as we approach the monastery. A finer quality of attention arises, like opening shutters to a clear morning light.

In Etna, the monks are expecting us. Archimandrite Akakios greets us with warm eyes and a humble, kind demeanor beneath his bushy blonde beard. He ushers us into the reception area and soon appears with a tray loaded down with glasses of cool mountain water, small shots of Ouzo and two decorated ceramic plates with three sweet cherries each. Another visitor, Joseph, introduces himself to us. He is a former counselor at a University and lives in Seattle. He and his wife Barbara have come for a visit. Archbishop Chrysostomos soon joins us. The nuns at St. Elizabeth the Grand Duchess convent have invited us for supper at 5:30 PM and then the Archbishop will receive us afterwards back at the monastery.

Archimandrite Akakios shares with us the joy of a recent event surrounding a Romanian Bishop known to the monks, who had suffered a great deal in the persecutions by the Communists under Romanian dictator, Nicolae Ceausescu, and had lived in virtual poverty. Metropolitan Cyprian had managed to purchase and present to him a fine Mercedes Benz car. A week before the anniversary of the glorification of St. Glycherie, the car was stolen by bandits who did not hurt the bishop. They took his money and the car and valuables. The police said the Bishop should be glad he was alive. "Such persons generally do not leave witnesses behind and it would be useless to even try and find the car. By now it is somewhere in Moscow."

A week later, on the day of the first anniversary of St. Glycherie's glorification, the bishop received news that the car, his wallet, papers and all the valuables were found in tact, parked along the street. It was a small miracle and the archimandrite wondered with a chuckle, "What must have happened to them in that car?!"

I find myself wondering what the event might have meant for the Bishop who had suffered so much in the persecutions and then suddenly received such unexpected largesse. What had he thought? Had he been willing to let go of the wonderful gift that he had been given? Was it like Jonah under the shade of the unpredictable plant? So often our problem is that we want to possess what is given and are not able to realize that God owns everything and allows us to use what we need. Why do we need to own something instead of remaining in partnership with God? Yet this disease lives within. It is strange anyone would trust our limited human control over the infinite divine capacity for gifting us all in love. A gift given to one, by God, is a gift given to all. How could it be otherwise? It seems so clear now. Why does this realization fade so quickly?

We talk for an hour or so and it is already after 5:30 PM. We are told the nuns will not be thrown off by our lateness. I apologize to them anyway when we arrive. Mother Justina greets Claudia and me and Joseph who has come with us. The Convent of St. Elizabeth the Grand Duchess is a small, beautiful white structure, cloistered behind a gate in the woods about five miles outside of town. The gold turrets atop the Chapel stand out brightly giving it a kind of magical feel. Walking through those gates we have entered a sanctuary of Grace and hospitality that is a living icon of Christ.

Mother Justina is soft-spoken and alert with that simplicity that is born of freedom from the dullness and inattention of worldly life, television and surfeit. She shows us the inside of the chapel and tells the story of St. Elizabeth, the granddaughter of Queen Victoria whose husband was murdered in front of her and she herself was later kidnapped and murdered after founding a monastery. The icons in the chapel are all rendered in fine detail by the nuns and are very beautiful. They also do hand embroidery of vestments and make prayer ropes. Everything evidences tender loving care and attention to every detail, from the chapel to the garden, to the refectory.

Mother Elizabeth, the abbess, is an earthy and genuine woman, a convert from the Methodist Church. She tells of how she came to be affected by the kindness of the monks during a difficult period in her life and how she was deeply impressed by the fact that "they *really* believe."

The food is simple and delicious —garden salad with fresh green peas and lettuce also from the convent garden, shrimp and garlic kabobs from the grill with spiced rice and vegetables. Every course is served by the nuns with the same quiet kindness, humility and reserve that was evidenced by Fr. Akakios. I feel grateful in my heart and very aware of the presence of my own arrogance and pride by contrast. This is another gift of such hospitality for which I am grateful. My ego is brought into clear relief by the unselfish, cheerful service of the monks and nuns who treat us like we are royalty, without a trace of interest in tickling our vanity or indulging any sort of self-importance, expecting nothing in return. What would we feel if we each went out of our way to treat the other with such kindness daily, serving one another's needs quietly without fanfare? One of my former professors, Robert Wicks, told how someone once said of Archbishop Tutu, "I know he is a holy man."

"How do you know this?" his friend asked.

"I know because when I am with him I feel holy."

Following dinner, the archbishop sends word that he will see Claudia and me for a talk. After some delicious freshly made strawberry short-cake covered with fresh strawberries from the convent garden, we return to St. Gregory's where we meet with His Eminence Archbishop Chrysostomos. The archbishop picked up where we had left off in our earlier conversation regarding the "distillation of Orthodoxy" from its ethnic roots.

The archbishop related a story of his spiritual father Metropolitan Cyprian, who told him of a monk who once confessed to him that he had been pure and not participated in "any of those sexual sins." The metropolitan was thinking later about the man and something was troubling him about his attitude, but he could not put his finger on it. Years later, he had occasion to hear the man's confession again, this time on his death bed. The monk at first would not allow him to place the *epitrachelion*[1] over him and hear his confession because "I have fallen." He told of a nun who had ministered to him in illness and how he and the nun had had sexual relations. He felt he could not be forgiven for this sin after so many years of honoring his vows. The metropolitan realized that the sin was God's means of bringing the man's pride to light so that he could be healed. In fact he was able to repent and ended his life well. The nun, had some kind of stroke and didn't even remember what had happened. Such is the

[1] The long stole worn around the neck of the priest when hearing confessions. It is placed over the penitent's head and the sign of the cross is made after the prayers of forgiveness are read.

mystery and kindness of God's clemency and provision for the cure of the human soul.

After our talk, I walked out under the canopy of stars blanketing the sky and I lay on top of one of the sarcophagi outside the monastery, staring up at endless expanse of heavens, praying the Jesus prayer and thanking God for such blessings on the trip and in my life. A softened grateful heart looks out upon a beautiful world of immense depth and drinks it in as from God's invisible hand. There are no words. I am thirsty now with a thirst that grows in direct proportion to awareness of God being forever out of reach, but yearned for because of feeling God close enough to be the thirst itself.

The following morning Divine Liturgy is at 8 AM, lasting about an hour and a half. Breakfast is served twenty minutes or so later; some boiled wheat *kollyva*, a banana, tea and bread. I noticed that Joseph and I were the only ones with bananas and silently offered half of mine to the young monk beside me but he motioned, "no."

Throughout the quickly eaten breakfast, one of the brothers stood in the pulpit above the refectory quietly praying the Jesus prayer out loud, pausing for ten to fifteen seconds between each refrain. The alternating of silence and the prayer stirred my attention. I remember the gift of each moment in the face of certain eventual death. For long moments in between I lose my way along the labyrinth of my life and am suddenly recalled to attention. God is present. Where am I? Where did I go in between such moments? How do I lose the thread of relationship which God gives me in this tender absence, finding a concept or a memory more interesting? *Lord, have mercy.*

The taste and smell of the food mingles with gratitude in my heart and I realize I am praying, eating and wondering simultaneously. *Lord Jesus Christ, have mercy on me.* Quietly. Steadily, with no trace of forcing, the monk prays the prayer at the pace of the pilgrimage he is living on a daily basis. Prayer enters into the whole experience without violence and awakens a kind of resonance. The monk is not on a mission. He is not trying to accomplish anything or make anything happen. Nor is he merely on vacation. He is present here and now. Simple. There is both attention and purpose, action and repose, as natural as breathing.

The act of eating and breathing in and releasing what God has provided to nourish life is itself a pilgrimage to the heart of faith woven out of strands of deep silence and guileless human presence. We are reborn with each inspiration and we die with each exhalation. In between there is the Grace of God acting, sufficient to shepherd us and call us gently into a life that cannot be lived by any sort of rushing or grasping. There is but one narrow way that corresponds exactly to a yoke made especially for each of us. Its departure and return are to the eternal present, linking us to the Divine life and to our human lives in the moment wherever we are, whatever we are doing.

Following breakfast, we leave the monastery with gifts in heart and hand: a bottle of sweet red Mavrodaphne wine from Greece and a block of garlic-infused feta cheese from the monastery goats — a gift from Bishop Auxentius. Claudia and I agree that this monastery cheese is without doubt the best we have ever eaten. Archbishop Chrysostomos gives Claudia a delicate white marble vase, hand turned in Romania where he'd been on pilgrimage sometime earlier. I ask to have my picture taken with the monks and he agrees, though demurring at first, saying "Pictures are for famous people." I remember Tony Campolo's comment, "God has each of our pictures in His wallet and takes them out and shows them off constantly." With God, we are each already famous. When he looks at us, he sees us as we are through the lens of His beloved Son.

It feels so good to be reminded how we are loved and cared for. Joy, humility and the unsentimental hospitality of our hosts reveal my sins and the coarseness, selfishness and fragmentation in me far more effectively than any amount of scolding or criticism ever could. This is an unintentional gift of the faithfulness of the monks and nuns, a byproduct of their genuine commitment to their own pilgrimages of obedience to Christ. Crumbs from their spiritual table have been a sumptuous feast for Claudia and me. Miraculously in the face of joy and love offered to me the unworthy sinner, I recognize the invisible depth of my own spiritual sickness. *Lord, have mercy on me a sinner.*

For a moment, the words of the prayer are enlivened by the wellsprings of the heart and they give renewed purpose to my life. St. Seraphim's words are indeed true, 'Find inner peace and acquire the Holy Spirit and thousands around you will attain salvation." We feasted not only on their excellent prayer-saturated food, but drank from the quietness and unaffectedness of their presence as well, quenching a thirst we often are not even aware of having until we stand in front of the only kind of water that can quench it — a water that wells up unto eternal life.

Setting off on the vacation part of our journey to the Oregon coast now, the bright greens and blues and the sweet air of the vibrant world spreading out around us is experienced as an extension of God's hospitality to those God loves. We are included. In the context of pilgrimage, the world is more beautiful than it ever is when my vacation is a mission to achieve satisfaction merely of my own pleasure and designs. Spiritual hunger and thirst arise from a place deeper than physical hunger. God has provided far more than we could even take in. Our cup runneth over. For a brief time, the world is infused with a capacity to ignite a quiet joy from every direction of our senses, reminding us of the heart of our marriage, a mystery where God's love dwells. United in this way, we are freed to love one another, and enjoy everything around us, because each of us is loved; to be generous with one another, because God has lavishly gifted the entire world. We are home.

Questions for Discussion

1. How do I give thanks at mealtime? Does God want me to include as prayer, tasting the essences in the food I eat at meals? Is consciousness of eating a sacred act? Is my presence and conversation with others anchored in inner attentiveness that offers nourishment to others around me through the quality of my presence?

2. Knowing that you will die one day and must let go of everything and everyone you have ever loved in the world, what makes it possible (or not) for you to feel at home in your life here now?

3. Are there times during the day that you could combine your ordinary activities with saying the Jesus prayer and intentional presence toward God? How do you think this might transform your life and affect others around you? Do you make this as important as brushing your teeth, balancing your checkbook and making sure there is oil in your car? If not why not?

In the Garden of the Panaghia

Every day is a journey, and the journey itself is home.

Basho

When faith is completely replaced by creed, worship by
discipline, love by habit; when the crisis of today is ignored
because of the splendor of the past; when faith becomes
an heirloom rather than a living fountain; when religion
speaks only in the name of authority rather than with the
voice of compassion — its message becomes meaningless.

Abraham Joshua Heschel

STARS ARE ABUNDANT IN THE NIGHT SKY OVER
the mountain outside the city of Patras, overlooking the
Ionian Sea. George, a retired engineer is wrapping our
water bottles in newspapers as he packs them in the
trunk to keep them cold. We are waiting for his brother,
Metropolitan Alexios, to join us for an all-night drive to
the northern corner of Greece. There, the monastic republic of Mount Athos lies on the outermost finger of the
Halkidiki Peninsula jutting out into the Aegean Sea.

My son Greg and I have arrived in Greece two days
before and had one good night's sleep in three days. Careening from one end of the Greek coast to the other

Edited from article published in *The Pastoral Forum*. Vol. 22 (1),
2007, pp. 10–14.

around hairpin turns, wedged shoulder to shoulder in the
back seat of the small six-cylinder European model Mercedes, I nibble on dried ginger root to manage the nausea.
Some eight hours later we arrive in the small coastal village of Ierissos in the early morning hours, waiting for an
uncertain boat ride to the eastern shore of Mount Athos,
the spiritual heart of the Orthodox Christian world.

Affectionately called the "garden of the Panaghia,"[1]
Mount Athos has been a protected, isolated pan-Ortho-
dox monastic enclave since the ninth century. It may have
been occupied by monks and hermits as early as the fourth
century when Emperor Constantine is said to have built
a church on the spot where the Monastery of Vatopaidi
now stands. When I first caught sight of the thousand year
old Byzantine monastery, bustling with signs of renewal,
ripe with fruits and flowers of all kinds and young monks
with flowing beards as black as their robes, any vestige of
physical misery faded like magic into the background. My
eyes and heart were alert, filling with something pristine
and unfathomable. I was on soil where the last surviving
remnants of the Byzantine Empire still evidence a world
as it was before shopping malls, environmental toxins and
the superficialities of modernity displaced Christian spirituality as the pulse and heartbeat of civilization.

Upon our arrival, traveling as guests of our metropolitan, who early in his life had been a monk here, we
were invited behind the altar of the church to venerate

---

[1] Meaning "The All Holy One," a reverential name for the Virgin Mary
made holy by the indwelling Grace of the God-man Jesus Christ.

the relics which include one of Emperor Constantine's wooden crosses from the early fourth century and most precious of all, the *zonē* or belt of the Panaghia — possibly the only surviving article in the world that once belonged to Jesus' mother who gave it to the Apostle Thomas. It remained in Jerusalem until the fourth century when it was removed by Emperor Arcadius who took it to Constantinople. Made of camel's hair believed to have been woven by the Theotokos[2] herself, it is associated with many miracles including the healing of Empress Zoe, the wife of Leo VI. Out of gratitude for her restored health, she embroidered it with gold threads which remain to this day. Some 30,000 people had come out to venerate it when it was taken outside the monastery in the weeks before our arrival. Several years later when the monks brought the precious relic to Moscow, Russians waited in line eight people wide stretching two to three kilometers for 28 hours to venerate the belt for only a few seconds.

It is said that on Mount Athos even the stones breathe prayers. Grace has a sheer kind of thickness here. Silence is the most ancient tongue the heart recognizes as its own, lost when the Garden was lost. An unspoken receptivity arises born of faith. We are on Byzantine time here. That means that midnight is regarded as the time of "sunset" and by reckoning of the Julian calendar, we are 13 days behind the rest of the world. In reality time here is set more by eternity, parsed by the ancient cycle

---

[2] Literally, "God-bearer."

of prayer, worship, and work that punctuates day and night in a rhythmical pattern. As I kissed the reliquary box containing the Virgin Mother's belt, I felt Grace releasing tears of joyful sorrow from deep within me. The Lord's mother is always in some way pointing us to her Son in whose presence no words suffice. A few minutes later, Hegumen[3] Ephraim's gentle presence sitting with us around the ancient stone table in the refectory seems like a living icon of the Lord emanating quiet joy and humility. He hands me a zucchini.

"From Vatopaidi," he says quietly, with a sweet smile. Tears brim my eyes as my heart receives this gift as from Jesus himself. A few minutes later the same with a tomato…and an onion.

"From Vatopaidi," he smiles, not the least bit disturbed or surprised by my tears. I am deeply grateful as I find myself responding to this quiet simple attention and generosity which touches me profoundly. And so it is again and again throughout several days on the Holy Mountain. *Everything* is iconic. I who deserve nothing am given everything as a gift from the Lord's hand and a blessing from His mother whose presence in her "garden" is also palpable. Without warning, at the darting of a swallow speeding by the balcony overlooking the ocean beyond the cypress trees where St. Gregory Palamas once had his hermitage, or bowing before the swing of a censor in the darkened incense-filled church surrounded

---

[3] The spiritual leader of the monastery to whom all monks are obedient.

by glowing ancient icons — at any moment suddenly the
heart burns, opening like a flower and the stones beneath
your feet become the road to Emmaus. You weep quietly
from the depths of your soul with gratitude and wonder.
It is more than words can express, yet so simple and viv-
idly clear. There is peace in the soul. Lest you think it is
anything you are doing or anything you are, another elder from Gregoriou Monastery reminds a few days later,
"Even prayer itself is a gift."

As we were leaving the refectory filing by Abbot
Ephraim for his blessing, he said to me, "Stephanos, I am
glad to meet you. I will pray for you." Once again I felt
grateful tears of appreciation for the gift of his personal
welcome which conveyed the welcome of Christ.

I noticed all the monks heading back into the church
and was not aware of there being another service. I followed, but when I saw only monks and no visitors inside, I thought it must be a talk just for the monks, so I
left. Anyway, I wanted to be alone to pray and I walked
up into a section in the center of a group of buildings
where Metropolitan Alexios had earlier pointed out he
had once stayed when he was a monk at Vatopaidi. Looking around to make sure I was alone, I turned inward and
prayed "Holy Theotokos help me!" over and over, asking
strongly in my heart that I might see her, while my mind
reminded me it was too much to ask.

Suddenly at just this moment, I became aware of a
young man walking up to me from my left. I wondered
how he had approached without me noticing. He was

dressed all in a vivid blue color, not as a monk, but in pants and shirt and he spoke to me in a language I was not familiar with. I said, "I speak English." He then changed to English with an accent and asked if I knew when the special service was starting? I said I didn't know anything about it. Without breaking his stride, he continued, "The service is for Miryam in ten minutes." Then he repeated it with emphasis. "It is for MIRYAM!" I walked back toward the church as the meaning of what he was saying began to dawn on me.

Inside I discovered an unexpected celebration already in process as the monks were preparing a replica of an icon of the Theotokos and Christ that was being given to St. Panteleimon Monastery by Vatopaidi. Bells were ringing and incense was flowing with the monks' robes as we all walked out in procession carrying aloft the huge icon into the parking lot to load it into the waiting van. Joy and gratitude to be part of this spontaneous event spread in me and then my mind began slowly pondering what had just happened.

As we stopped and gathered outside the monastery gate, I looked around as I had done in the church, trying to find the man in blue. He was nowhere to be found. Why had he called her Miryam? That seemed to me a kind of informal intimacy and somewhat unorthodox for a monk. My mind turned over what I had experienced. I remembered the man's unusually bright countenance and a perfectly clear complexion that had a wholesomeness to it that was unusual almost like it was deliberately understated yet its uniqueness not totally disguised. He had asked me when the special service was and then when I didn't know, *he told me*. He repeated himself twice, emphasizing the name "Miryam" until I comprehended that his response was the answer to my unspoken prayer. If I wanted to see the Holy Theotokos, she was about to appear.

Where had he come from? Standing in the middle of a large square having made sure I was alone, at the *exact* moment I was praying 'Holy Theotokos help me!" on the prayer rope, and asking her to appear to me, I discover him walking toward me. He is seemingly intent on going to the church, yet he never arrives.

Tears came up from deep within as my heart entertained the strange possibility that the man was an angel. If not an otherworldly being, he was nevertheless a messenger in physical form sent from the Holy Theotokos in immediate answer to my prayer, directing me to her in the church!

I was bent over a small bridge apart, weeping, undone by a mixture of joy, sadness and shame at being unworthy of such a gift yet so immensely grateful. From the periphery of my mind, the psychotherapist observer was wondering if I was imagining things in order to "have an experience." How narcissistic to think such a thing might have occurred for me. When Metropolitan Alexios came over and asked me what was wrong, I could not stop weeping as I tried to tell him I could not find the man who had spoken to me these things. I asked him to tell Abbot Ephraim that I felt I had encountered an angel.

After a moment he came back and said, "The abbot responded, "It frequently happens that God helps pilgrims in such ways." Simple. In the world of Athos, the ordinary is extraordinary and the extraordinary is ordinary. All is gift. No one is worthy, yet all are beloved.

What do we have in this world that is not gift in just this way, and yet we do not recognize and appreciate it as miraculous? Faith is not only the "assurance of things unseen"[4] but gratefulness for a dimension of the things that are seen which we would otherwise take for granted. How often am I given something and never understand its real meaning? Paradoxically, my own life is not really mine as long as I imagine in my hubris that it is or that I am master of my fate. It has been given at great price through the "Lamb slain from the foundation of the world" as a kind of seed to be planted sacrificially in the existential soil of time and space so that the world might have life and have it abundantly. Thou, O Lord, are the "Treasury of blessings and Giver of life." Spiritually sober for a moment, you begin to comprehend as did the Apostle Paul, that in reality "It is no longer I but Christ who lives in me"[5] and for whom I live, recognized in all people everywhere in all places and in all living things. The mystery of love is that we are each distinct and yet one body. Where love exists my neighbor *is* myself. I cannot become myself apart from the same love for the world as God has for me. Our fate is bound together.

---

[4] Hebrews 11:1.
[5] Gal. 2:20.

What is it that prevents me from recognizing and living this precious miracle day to day, of receiving everything, every single particle of creation as from the Lord's own hand just as it is offered and becoming responsible for being a good steward of it all? What greater miracle do I need to awaken both joy and responsibility than grateful awareness of each breath that is given? Such love seems more than I can bear and yet I know beyond doubt that it is something I cannot truly live without.

This awareness of Grace is the gift of the "Holy Mountain" to the world and its humble elders are its spiritual heartbeat. Mount Athos is a beacon lighting the way of ancient Christianity whose spirit is unchanged from the first century, born of the Uncreated Grace found in the mystery of Eucharist, in hesychia, the *stillness* of continual prayer of the heart, and in the monks' daily hospitality to strangers. Love, humility, joy, peace, repentance, prayer, worship, healing, hospitality and community are fruits of the Spirit that are drawing new life into Mount Athos and overflowing the cups of pilgrims who bring their spiritual longing to its shores, now limited to no more than 40,000 a year. Perhaps no other community on earth in the last two millennia has shared communal life between humankind, nature and the spiritual world for as long in the same traditional way without being fatally corrupted or destroyed. Like everything precious it must be protected so that it can continue to offer this special nourishment to a world in great need of its sobering refreshment. As one frequent pilgrim and former president of the Friends of Athos Society observed:

The exclusiveness of Athos is essential to its survival. If it were to be compromised, there is no doubt
that within a very short space of time the sole surviving holy mountain would suffer the same fate as
others, like Meteora and countless other monasteries in Greece and the Middle East that are now ei-
ther museums of Byzantine art or deserted ruins.[6]

Or mere tourist stops bereft of spiritual vitality. In-
terestingly, it has seemed at times, to secular observers
focusing on the surface of things, as though this might
already be imminent, that the peculiar culture of Athos
might not survive. Only a quarter of a century ago, young
men were not coming, the ancient fortress-like buildings
were in disrepair and Byzantine culture seemed increasingly irrelevant to a technologically advancing modern
world. Writing in 1966, an English visitor wrote, "Athos
is dying — and dying fast. Probably within the lifetime
of most readers the thousand year history of the Holy
Mountain (will) come to an end. The disease is incurable.
There is no hope."[7]

Thankfully he could not have been more wrong. Subsequent years have shown God's hidden hand at work
fructifying the seeds of renewal. The Panaghia has not
abandoned her garden which is attracting young univer-
sity-educated men with doctoral-level training as physi-

---

[6] Graham Speake. *Mount Athos: Renewal in Paradise* (New Haven
and London: Yale University Press, 2002), p. 264.
[7] Ibid., p. 4.

cians, engineers and theologians. Significantly, their deep spiritual thirst is being quenched at the wells of men who have lived in caves since the age of nineteen, spending their whole lives in prayer. In this way the ancient traditional path remains, while integrating aspects of modern life shorn of whatever is not compatible with the Pearl of Great Price. But how is this possible?

One answer is the spiritual obedience, selfless service and discernment of a variety of grace-filled elders, educated in the "University of the desert" by the Holy Spirit, each with his own unique and distinctly original presence, renewed by the same artesian waters of Grace activating continual prayer and repentance and imbuing them with humility, sobriety, joy and discernment that makes them virtual spiritual magnets for those in search of authentic Christian life.

In the 1950's, a small group of men hidden from the world's eyes formed a brotherhood around the remarkable cave dweller, Elder Joseph the Hesychast, who conveyed to them the deep mysteries of Grace-impelled continual prayer of Jesus which had been given to him miraculously by the Holy Theotokos after long spiritual labors.[8] Three of these men went on to become abbots of monasteries on Mount Athos, converting them from their previous deteriorating idiorrhythmic status (where monks are permitted to own private property and set their own rules of life), to coenobitic monasteries shar-

---

[8] Elder Joseph. *Elder Joseph the Hesychast* (Mount Athos: Holy Monastery of Vatopaidi, 1999).

ing a life in common where all are spiritually obedient to the hegumen or abbot. One of these men, Elder Ephraim, also began several women's monasteries in Greece, before eventually responding to the Holy Spirit's call to North America where he has begun seventeen thriving monasteries,[9] for both men and women, the largest of which is in the Sonoran desert in Arizona and follows the Athonite *typikon*.[10]

Seeds of revival were sewn at the Monasteries of Stavronikita and later Iviron with the arrival of Elder Vasileios Gontikakis, whose writings are among the most beautiful and inspiring produced from Athos in the last quarter century. His description of a mature monk might well serve as a general description of an elder in the making:

> Coming into contact with a monk who has reached maturity, one finds nothing superhuman in him, nothing that astonishes or makes one giddy, but rather something deeply human and humble, something that brings peace and new courage. Despite his asceticism, despite his separation from the world, he is not in reality cut off from persons. On the contrary, he has returned to them, he has embraced all people in their suffering and has become truly human.[11]

---

[9] Two are in Canada and fifteen are in the United States.

[10] Pattern of rules governing the worship and life of a monastery.

[11] Archimandrite Vasileios. "Conference of Archimandrite Vasileios" in S. Bolshakoff (Ed). *In Search of True Wisdom* (1974), p. 127.

Another remarkable elder, Aimilianos, left Meteora with a number of monks devoted to him as their spiritual leader in order to get away from the distraction of heavy tourism and was welcomed as Abbot of the Monastery of Simonopetra. Years before, he had consulted the spiritually gifted Elder Ephraim of Katounakia (who also had Elder Joseph as his spiritual guide) concerning mental prayer. After Abbot Aimilianos had left, Elder Ephraim's disciple remembers the clairvoyant elder saying

"Let's pray and see what kind of person this man is." Having done so, he remarked, "This man, my child, is like fragrance."[12]

On another trip, Fr. Athanasios, who had come from Meteora to Simonopetra Monastery with Fr. Amilianos forty years earlier, told us how once when Elder Ephraim of Kaotounakia visited their monastery, the monks noticed him stagger into the church, dazed, while Elder Amilianos was serving at the altar. After the Liturgy, the two of them went into a room together by themselves and talked for four hours. The monks later discovered that Elder Ephraim had seen Elder Amilianos transfigured and the Spirit of love like a light was hovering above the heads of all the monks.

Not only did Elder Aimilianos revive Simonopetra monastery, but he went on to develop what is now the largest women's monastery in Greece at Ormylia — a Mount Athos outside Athos, where worship, spiritual direction,

---

[12] Tessy Vassiliadou-Christodoulou. *Elder Ephraim of Katounakia* (Mount Athos: Monastery of Katounakia, 2003), p. 97.

pastoral care, social services and the highest quality medical treatment for breast cancer is offered in an integrated way, all free of charge as a gift to the people. This fulfills the edict of one of the early ecumenical councils which tasked every bishop with starting a hospital which was to be an integrated system of care infused by the Christian mystery. Over a hundred fifty thousand women have been screened for cancer through the initiatives of the Panaghia Philanthropini Monastery at Ormylia, evidencing the power of Orthodox Christian spirituality to fulfill the call to unite modern scientific technologies with the ancient truth of Christian faith in philanthropic service of humanity in a seamless way.

It is noteworthy that *all* of the thriving monasteries have found new life as coenobitic communities with spiritual obedience to a grace-filled elder along with continual inner prayer and hospitality to pilgrims as the heart of their endeavors. By contrast to the upside down kingdom of the world dominated by the marketplace, they fulfill the wisdom of the Lord's injunction to "Seek first the Kingdom of Heaven ..." and all the rest of the things that are truly needful in life will be added unto us in proper measure. They remind us that the vision and health of every community depends on its relationship to its spiritual center, just as the same is true for each person.

This is especially significant in our modern context where the psychology of self-esteem can suck the air out of any mention of ascetical self-denial. Anxieties over economic growth and expansion easily eclipse the mission of self-emptying, loving service to others, including responsibility for protecting the carrying capacity of the environment we all share for future generations. Athos is a testimony of how community life can endure for millennia creating conditions for persons to become fully alive, so long as worship of God, responsibility for intentional continuous prayer and hospitality to strangers is at the core over everything.

God-esteem is infinitely more precious and life-giving than mere self-esteem. St. Ireneaus, who sat at the feet of St. Polycarp who learned from the Apostle John who knew the Lord Jesus Christ firsthand, once observed "The glory of God is a human being fully alive." The One most fully alive is remembered by the Apostles as saying, "Come to Me all of you who labor and are heavy laden and I will give you rest for I am meek and lowly and my burden is light."[13] Jesus emptied Himself so that humanity might come to dwell completely within Him.

D. W. Winnicot is said to have observed, "When the therapist is reacting, there is no room for the client's mind." In the same way, it can be said that the kenotic[14] stillness of the elder's being is what draws us toward the true self which is always 'hid with Christ in God' beyond the constraints of self-judgment or diagnosis from the outside. The authentic self is called forth in loving relationship where there is total freedom from coercion

---

[13] Mt. 11:29.

[14] *Kenosis* refers to the self-emptying of egotism that is the source of making room for the other in love.

or manipulation of any kind. Paradoxically, I "become myself" as one elder suggested, when "I am no longer interested in myself, but only in what Christ is doing." Such persons are true spiritual physicians and lovers of humankind. Illumined by the Holy Spirit, they see and feel and hear a person's deep soul suffering clearly in the emptiness of a heart rendered free from the passions and distractions of self-will. Theirs is a condition quite opposite of being "full of myself." It is not that they have no self, but that the self is given them by God through the action of selfless love in a mysterious and secret way "where the left hand does not know what the right hand is doing." The elder's wisdom is more from the wellspring of childlike unknowing and trust in faith, than from any sort of egoistic surety of accumulated knowledge, information or even worldly experience, though none of these in and of themselves are scorned.

The Holy Spirit speaks softly from the place in the heart where it is said that we as sheep hear and will respond from the depths only to the shepherd's voice.[15] The sheep may be startled and even manipulated by other voices, but they will not *listen*. They will not *become free*. They will not find peace in their souls. The heart does not well up into a spring of living water when called to by a voice which does not issue forth from love that lays down its life for the sheep. The farther we move from personal relationship with the Living God and harmony with the

---

[15] Jn. 10:27.

organic natural world and the larger community of all human life that is an integral part of it, the thicker the insulation that binds us into our own private hells, and no human-derived philosophy, psychotherapy or technology is powerful enough to remedy this.

God is love. This much is clear. Whatever else we may say about Christian maturity, in the final analysis it is simply love flowing from the cross upon which the self bears crucifixion so that others may be free to live. This is the source of the spiritual charisma that is renewing life on Mount Athos and is fully capable of doing so in the churches and in the world if only we will allow it. The greatest adventure of life is to become obedient to God who *is* love; to make this the aim from the moment my eyes open in the morning to the seconds before they close at night.

A quiet and deep soul once reminded me wistfully, "Love is an endless interrogation." We are forever repenting of failing to be able to love as God loves us. The real tragedy is not to have experienced this failure. But as G. K. Chesterton once quipped, "It is not that Christianity has failed, but that it has proved too difficult for us to even try."

Questions for Discussion

1. What makes a pilgrimage different than a vacation? Am I a pilgrim in my life on a daily basis? What am I watching and listening for each day, that confirms my pilgrimage?

2. Am I receiving what is given to me in my life as something I have earned or am entitled too or as something given from God purely as a gift? Do my outer responses reflect gratefulness for life or taken-for-grantedness? What can I do to awaken thanksgiving for the gifts of each moment?

3. What is meant by "Love is an endless interrogation?" What is the evidence in my life that I am questioned by being endlessly loved by God? And what is my response?

Our Daily *Being* Bread

> It is the greatest mystery of life that satisfaction is felt not by those who take, and make demands, but by those who give, and make sacrifices. In them alone the energy of life does not fail, and this is precisely what is meant by creativeness... If you want to receive, give; if you want to obtain satisfaction, do not seek it, never think of it, and forget the very word; if you want to acquire strength, manifest it, give it to others.
>
> *Nicholas Berdyaev*

THE PICTURE CHOSEN FOR THE COVER OF THIS book is a photograph I stumbled upon while on the boat Axios Estin, travelling from the village of Ouranopolis, Greece en route to the port of Daphne on the peninsula of Halkidiki known as the monastic republic of Mount Athos.

I had noticed one of the monks feeding the gulls trailing along behind, something I love to do, enjoying the connection with creatures that are not interested in my personality, yet will relate to me through something real and immediate. All wild animals are vital to humanity in this regard, offering an essential encounter with the 'other' that is based not on egotism, but purely on concrete, embodied action and presence. Wild creatures see what we are in the moment and are not impressed by who we pretend to be or think we are in our imaginations. They respond to what is. They help us awaken to the sensation of ourselves — an essential ingredient of presence.

I tried several times to get a picture which might capture what I imagined in my mind to be a representation of the Trinitarian mystery of Father, Son and Holy Spirit being symbolized in this simple interaction, in the form of the monastic father, with the white gull as 'dove' and the Eucharistic presence of Christ's body in the form of the bread offered for the life of the world. Flung from the priest's hand into the waiting mouth of the gull in flight, it brought to mind the Psalmist's praise to "the Lord who gives the beasts their food and feeds the young ravens when they cry."[1]

I liked how the picture turned out, with the monk's hand forming his fingers in that special way which is done to give the priestly blessing, making each of the Greek letters, ICXC, signifying "Jesus Christ." But when I got home and had the picture enlarged I noticed something even more significant. It took my breath away, rendering the photograph a message from a depth for which I am always grateful and in awe for the smallest crumb. What I found unexpectedly present rendered the picture a perfect representation for this collection of glimmerings of Divine gifts that chronicle the small ways God's invisible hand in the world reveals itself gratuitously and personally in our lives in unexpected and subtle ways. More than that, it revealed a dimension all too easily overlooked, that is the ground for the possibility of our daily *being* bread.

During the invocation to the Holy Spirit in the Divine Liturgy, the priest separates the "lamb"[2] into four

---

[1] Psalm 147:9.

[2] This is the name given to the piece of bread that is cut from the

quarters on the discus, making the shape of the cross. While offering prayers, he will place the top portion in the Chalice containing the red wine. Then pouring in *zeon* (hot water) accompanied by the words, "the warmth of the Holy Spirit," in preparation for serving the Holy Eucharist. He will consume a part of the second piece and place the rest in the chalice.

If you look closely at the picture, you can see floating on the water directly beneath the morsel suspended at a moment in the air, four fragments of bread which are in the shape of the cross in just that way as they are separated by the priest on the discus during every Divine Liturgy at precisely that moment before he himself consumes a piece and places the others in the Chalice for the Eucharist. The priest is nourished by the Bread of Life which is given to us through the cross so as to ready himself to offer this bread to each of us. Without the cross, there is no bread. Without bread, there is no life. Without the person of Christ who unites heaven and earth, we have no *being*.

The snap of the camera lens occurred at just that moment in which there was an unseen message (and Messenger!) to be discovered and deciphered later, reminding that behind every Eucharistic offering of the Divine

---

heart of the *prosphora*, the bread baked and given for use in the Liturgy each Sunday, by one of the members of the church. The letters IXNIKA (Jesus Christ Conquers) are baked into the surface of the bread, and a lance, symbolizing the spear used to pierce the Lord's heart on the cross, is used to cut this from the loaf. This is the "lamb" that is used in the "bloodless" sacrifice on the altar.

Liturgy that stirs our hearts, behind every gift great and small, is hidden the mysterious deep pathos of the cross of Christ cast upon the waters of chaos, as upon an altar, at the beginning of Creation. As the dove once hovered over the waters at the second re-creation following the flood, and yet again at the third re-creation following the baptism of Jesus in the Jordan — all are echoes of the "Lamb slain from the foundation of the world."[3] The picture is a confirmation of the relationship between the "One who offers and the One who is offered."[4] Wherever we feed one another and care for the smallest of God's creatures, we ourselves are fed in the process. Love is a reciprocal breathing, a circle of compassion.

Christ's gift of Himself to the world as the daily bread of our *being* evidences a dialogical reciprocity that carries with it so potent an invitation beyond our human power alone, that we like his Apostles who fall asleep in the Garden during the Lord's Gethsemane agony, find it impossible to bear and respond to it in our daily lives for the same reasons. Like persons suffering from the dissociation and numbing of post-traumatic stress, we too find ourselves seeking to avoid our own martyrdom by losing ourselves in our daily routines and comfortable lives. Life becomes a place to hide in unconsciousness rather than to be consciously lifted up as the royal priesthood who stand in the presence of God's glory.

---

[3] Rev. 13:8.
[4] From the Divine Liturgy.

Yet, it is precisely the witness (the Greek word *martyr* literally means "witness") of those who have consumed His pure Body and Precious Blood in the Eucharist, through whom the blood of Christ now flows, that can offer the clearest testimony to the world of the reality of God's love. It is this action of becoming bread for the life of the world that is continued through His disciples which constitutes the true life of the Church and gives meaning to Tertullian's saying: "The blood of the martyrs is the seed of the Church."[5] The Church is not a building or a ritual, but the eternal call and response whereby we enter freely and joyfully into the invitation "Thy will be done on earth as it is in heaven." This is the relationship between God and the royal priesthood of all humanity that is the divine cosmic Liturgy[6] of life.

The reciprocity of love experienced through Christ in this way reveals God the Father's wish to invite created persons into the Uncreated life of the Holy Trinity as much more than Jesus substituting Himself for us so that we need not follow the Way Jesus follows. Christ bids each of us "follow me" into God's heart. This is the invitation to eternal life which entices, troubles and confuses us as it did the Apostles who wisely and mercifully left us the record of their failures in their memoirs.[7] As the days prior to His

[5] AD 160–220. According to tradition, Tertullian was trained as a lawyer and served as an ordained priest in the Church.

[6] Liturgy comes from the Greek word Λειτουργία, which translates as "work in behalf of the people."

[7] "Justin Martyr is the first writer to appeal to New Testament writing, which he refers to as " memoirs" (τὰ ἀπομνημονεύματα) of the apostles, which, he notes are called "Gospels" (First Apology

sacrifice came near, Jesus tried to prepare His Apostles for His departure saying "You know the place I am going." When He spoke of His coming self-offering, which they still found confusing, Thomas spoke up asking, "Lord we don't know where you are going, so how can we know the way?"[8] This should alert us to the fact that we who come after the apostles will also be troubled and confused by this when we face it in our lives, even though we proclaim "He is Risen!" with joy each Paschal celebration.

Jesus' response was strange. "I am the Way, the Truth and the Life and no one goes to the Father except through me."[9] Far from being an exclusion of those who "don't believe in Jesus" this statement points to the heart of life which is shared by all persons, whether realized or not. Because God's nature and human nature are seamlessly united in the person of Jesus, there is no way to encounter Eucharist except through the humbling crucifixion of individualistic self-love which makes room for the other in our own life. "I tell you the truth, unless a kernel of wheat falls to the ground and dies, it remains only a single seed. But if it dies, it produces many seeds."[10] In this sense, as Elder Thaddeus of Serbia says, "Our entire life on this earth itself is an *epitimion*"[11] which helps prepare us for the transformation

---

66:3)" St. Irenaeus of Lyons, trans. Fr. John Behr, *On the Apostolic Preaching* (New York: St. Vladimir's Seminary Press, 1997) 11.

[8] Jn. 14:5.

[9] Jn. 14:6.

[10] Jn 12:24.

[11] An *epitimion* is a penance offered for full cure after forgiveness is given in confession. Serbian Elder Thaddeus of Vitovnica sug-

through Grace into the "communion of otherness"[12] with all whom God loves. The mere fact that we are conditioned and God is unconditioned is enough to unsettle the waters of any encounter between the two.

Jesus said, "My food is to do the will of Him who sent me"[13] and he in turn is our food which enables us to do the will of the Father, "for it is no longer I but Christ who lives in me.[14]" It is in the world as the royal priesthood that we stand and serve before the altar of our neighbor's heart, newly illumined by receiving the *being* bread of Christ in the Liturgy.[15] Here we encounter Christ anew in a thousand forms and discover again the mystery that the One who offers is made visible through the One who is offered.

---

gests that our whole life on earth functions in this way. "He who does not sacrifice himself like a lamb to slaughter ... who does not shed blood in order to attain virtue — such a person will never attain virtue. God, by His Divine providence, has established it so: we attain eternal life by our voluntary death. If you will not die a voluntary death, you will not attain eternal life and you will be dead." Cf. Thaddeus, Elder. *Our Thoughts Determine Our Lives.* (California: St. Herman of Alaska Brotherhood, 2009) p. 137

[12] Cf. John D. Zizioulas. *Communion & Otherness* (London: T&T Clark, 2006) for an exploration of how the Trinity reveals the paradox of Communion of otherness — the otherness of all persons and the absolute Otherness of God and humanity.

[13] Jn. 4:34.

[14] Gal. 2:20.

[15] The Divine Liturgy is empty if not connected to existential relations between persons. We are shown this by the words of Jesus himself who according to Mt 5:24 tells the Apostles, "leave your gift there in front of the altar. First go and be reconciled to your brother; then come and offer your gift."

Jesus is the path leading into the διά-Λογος of Communion, the meeting between the uncreated and created worlds, an event more akin to the conjunction of matter and anti-matter.[16] As God told Moses on Sinai "If you look upon my Face you will die." Obliterated. Yet if we respond to Jesus from the heart with the eyes of faith we will discover at some point with St. Paul that "it is not longer I but Christ who lives in me."[17] We are then following the same road Jesus followed. The spiritual thermonuclear combustion of uniting God and creation is as powerfully traumatic to Jesus as it is potentially transformational and salvational for us. It is impossible for a human being on his or her own even to receive our daily *being* bread without God's help. Christianity is more than a difficult way. It is completely beyond human capacity. "The Way that leads to life is narrow. Few find it and fewer still enter in."[18] And yet it is offered freely to all, so that it has been said, "the only locks in hell are on the inside of the door."

The Gospels record only enough of Jesus' life on earth, his birth and bits and pieces of a few years of adult

---

[16] Outwardly nothing is visible; our life is such that nothing particular can be said about it. But inwardly, thanks to obedience, we are in a state of permanent tension. That is what a Christian should be: a high tension "cable" on which a little bird can perch without the least harm, yet through which passes an energy capable of blowing up the whole world. This is how we will gain entry to the eternal kingdom of Christ. Archimandrite Sophrony, *Words of Life* (Essex: Stavropegic Monastery of St. John the Baptist, 1996) pp. 37–38.

[17] Gal. 2:20.

[18] Mt. 7:14.

ministry, in order to illumine the meaning of His passion, death and resurrection. The "way" of Christ is captured well by Fr. Ernesto Cardenal when he writes, "Human beings are not a meaningless passion, but a passion whose meaning is God." This is the great secret spread out invisibly everywhere right before our eyes. Jesus is God's heart taking every person's heart of flesh as His own, so that God can raise us to eternal life, not by becoming superhuman, but like Him, by becoming fully human. This happens through the cross which is present in God's heart from the beginning, because as Fr. Lev Gillet points out: "There was a cross in the heart of God before there was one outside of Jerusalem."[19] And this mystery remains a choice in every human heart. Herein lies the heart-rending invitation and fathomless possibility of $\delta\iota\acute{\alpha}$-$\Lambda o\gamma o\varsigma$ between God and humankind which is the meaning of the terrible words, 'Take, eat. This is my body broken for you. This is my blood poured out for you. Drink of it, all of you."

Having received into ourselves the mystery of the super substantial bread, let us consider the result. "Thine own, of Thine own, we offer Thee, in all and for all"[20] that we might become bread for the world ourselves. This is the path of salvation offered every moment in the greater cosmic liturgy of our everyday lives and relationships. *Maranatha!*

---

[19] Lev Gillet, "Does God Suffer?", *Sobornost* 3:15 (1954), p. 120.
[20] From the Divine Liturgy of the Eastern Orthodox Church.

QUESTIONS FOR DISCUSSION

1. When we awaken we know we have been asleep. Describe a moment in your life when you awakened from the passive hypnotic dream of everyday life and found yourself aware of the people and the world around you in the presence of God in such a way that the ordinary took on a depth and meaning that evoked wonder, interest, gratitude and remorse.

2. Describe the experience of making a sacrifice for someone and contrast it with a time when you made a demand? Does God demand anything of you? What is your experience of God making a sacrifice for you?

3. What have I discovered about the relationship between receiving the Holy Eucharist and offering myself in loving service, becoming bread for the life of those around me? Am I ready to pray with my life, "Lord enable me to become eucharist with you, for the life of the world?"

Remember the writer of these pages in your prayers.
Lord Jesus Christ have mercy on me, the sinner.

About the Author

STEPHEN MUSE, PH.D., LMFT, LPC, B.C.E.T.S
is Co-Director responsible for the Pastoral Counselor
Training program and Clinical Services for the D.A &
Elizabeth Turner Ministry Resource Center of the Pastoral Institute, Inc. in Columbus, Georgia and teaches
and supervises in the U.S. Army Family Life Chaplain
Training program at Fort Benning. He has served as a
part time instructor in the graduate counseling program
of Columbus State University, as a clinical field supervisor for Auburn University counseling psychology program and as adjunct faculty with the doctoral programs
of Garrett Evangelical Seminary in Illinois and Union
Graduate Institute in Ohio.

Dr. Muse has taught and led professional workshops
throughout the U.S. and Internationally in the civilian
sector as well as for the U.S. Army Chaplains in the areas
of his specialties which include healing combat trauma &
abuse, training clergy as pastoral counselors, stress and

burn-out of clergy and helping professionals, Orthodox Christian life and spiritual formation, and Orthodox Christianity and marriage.

He has contributed chapters in eight books and more than 30 articles, book reviews and poetry for professional journals and trade magazines, including national award winning research in the area of religious integration and clinical empathy of therapists. His work has been translated into Russian, Greek, Swedish and Serbian. He served as Managing Editor of *The Pastoral Forum* from 1993 to 2002. Previous books include *Beside Still Waters: Restoring the Souls of Shepherds in the Market Place* (2000); *Raising Lazarus: Integral Healing in Orthodox Christianity* (2004), and *When Hearts Become Flame: An Eastern Orthodox Approach to the διά-Λογος of Pastoral Counseling* (2010).

Dr. Muse holds a bachelors degree in philosophy from Davidson College, an M.Div. from Princeton Theological Seminary emphasizing Greek New Testament exegesis and early church spirituality, M.S. and Ph.D. degrees from Loyola University of Maryland in Pastoral Counseling and has completed post graduate work in marriage and family studies through the University of Georgia. He holds Diplomate certification in the American Association of Pastoral Counselors; in Professional Psychotherapy with the International Academy of Behavioral Medicine, Counseling and Psychotherapy, and is an AAMFT Approved supervisor, Board certified in Traumatic Stress and in clinical hypnotherapy. He is licensed in the state of Georgia as both a Professional Counselor and a Marriage and Family Therapist and board certified as a life and clergy coach.

Prior to his reception into the Greek Orthodox Church where he is ordained as a Subdeacon and set apart for ministry as a pastoral counselor, Dr. Muse pastored a Presbyterian congregation for 11 years and helped begin an outpatient psychiatric clinic in Delta, PA. He is past president of the Orthodox Christian Association of Medicine, Psychology and Religion and a founding member and first parish council President of Holy Transfiguration Greek Orthodox Mission Church in Columbus. He and his wife Claudia have four children: a daughter killed in 1982, a daughter 34, a son 30, a daughter 29 and a granddaughter, 5 with another on the way.

Dr. Muse can be contacted at smuse@pilink.org.

CPSIA information can be obtained at www.ICGtesting.com
Printed in the USA
LVOW131150110313

323599LV00001B/1/P